WHITBY
An Extraordinary Town

by

Rosalin Barker

To Virginia,
A memento of an
enjoyable stay!
love, Simon
and Cline.

BLACKTHORN PRESS

Blackthorn Press, Blackthorn House
Middleton Rd, Pickering YO18 8AL
United Kingdom

www.blackthornpress.com

ISBN 978 1 906259 05 1

©Rosalin Barker 2007

Printed and bound by CPI Antony Rowe, Eastbourne

CONTENTS

PREFACE   *iv*

ACKNOWLEDGEMENTS   *v*

ILLUSTRATIONS   *vi*

FOUNDATIONS   *1*

NORMAN ABBEY AND MEDIEVAL TOWN   *11*

THE RIVER ESK   *24*

DOWN TO THE SEA IN SHIPS   *40*

WARS AND RUMOURS OF WARS   *58*

GOOD, BAD AND DESPERATE; THE HANDLING
OF MONEY   *68*

SCHOOLS AND SCHOLARS   *78*

ARTISTS, GEOLOGISTS AND LADY NOVELISTS   *84*

HOUSES AND PEOPLE OF GOD   *93*

EPILOGUE   *101*

FURTHER READING   *108*

INDEX   *109*

PREFACE

After the publication of the original *Book of Whitby*, I was surprised by the speed with which it sold out, and have been, over the intervening years, touched by the number of requests for a reprint.

Until recently that has not been not possible. However, now that I have been able to go back to the original book and think about another printing, I realised that to have considered just a reprint after so long would have been to neglect the amount of research I have been able to undertake into Whitby's complex history.

This, therefore is '*The Book of Whitby: Revised.*' To those who have read the original, there will be much that is familiar, but there will also be new material, and new considerations of my views in the original. I hope also that new publishing techniques will make it more accessible, and cost effective.

ACKNOWLEDGEMENTS

The author's nightmare is that someone will feel left out of the acknowledgements. Indeed, in a book such as this, it is almost certain that credit will be insufficiently given to one or other who has helped materially, if unknowingly. Any community with a history as rich as that of Whitby has a deep sense of its identity, and a great love of place, so that it is a topic often discussed, and it is from such discussions that many of the threads which have been followed have derived. I must therefore thank all those who have spoken to me, come to my lectures and classes, brought me snippets of information or copies of documents, read my articles and subsequently contacted me, and above all encouraged me.

Thanks are due; to the Hon. Keepers, and volunteer staff, of Whitby Museum, for the use of the library and the archives, and for illustrations; to the Sutcliffe Gallery and Whitby Literary and Philosophical Society for photographs by Frank Meadow Sutcliffe; to the late John Tindale for information; to the sometime Harbour-Master, Captain Peter Roberts, for his patience with my research about the harbour and to the Friends of Whitby Abbey.

There have been many who have helped me since the first edition, particularly my family for putting up with abstraction and piles of paper; patient archivists and librarians in the University of Hull, the Borthwick Institute, the National Archives, the British Library and North Yorkshire County Record Office and friends and colleagues in Hull and Whitby.

ILLUSTRATIONS IN THE TEXT

1. Lionel Charlton's map of Whitby 1778. *xi*

2. Part of the east pier and the east headland looking up to St Mary's church and the Abbey ruins. Much of the foreground of the east cliff has long since slid into the harbour and has recently been strengthened with 'rock armour'. (Frank Meadow Sutcliffe) *8*

3. The Spa ladder, called after an adjacent spring, connected the landward end of the East Pier to the end of Henrietta Street. It became too dangerous, and a new access has been created. The fishermen used the sides of the ladder, which was actually a suspended walk-way, for drying their nets. Nets and crab or lobster pots are still a familiar sight in various places round the harbour. (FMS) *9*

4. The 199 Church Stairs, which lead from Henrietta Street to St Mary's churchyard. Originally wooden, they have been much restored over many centuries and are currently undergoing more restoration. To the right is a smaller flight of steps and the cobbled roadway known as the 'donkey path'. (FMS) *10*

5. Rumburgh Priory; this Suffolk priory was founded in the 11th century by monks probably professed at Whitby; even this later four-square church would look more at home in Yorkshire. (Rosalin Barker) *20*

6. This the most familiar view of Whitby Abbey ruins, showing the Early English east end, with the mediaeval Abbey pond. (FMS) *21*

7. Market day, on the present market site, with the town hall and tollbooth in the background. Farmers and market-gardeners brought their produce into the town to sell. (FMS) *22*

8. Argument's Yard, 'Argument' being a local surname. The yards ran between the medieval streets, with steps to accommodate Whitby's steep contours, and houses later built behind and on top of each other to maximise living space in the restricted burgage. (FMS) *23*

9. This photograph taken from the churchyard shows the early development of the piers. The medieval Burgess Pier can be seen in the left foreground and was the original east pier. On the opposite bank by the bandstand can be seen seventeenth century developments to protect coal staithes to the left. (RRB) *31*

10. This shows the later pier development, including that of 1702, when Whitby became a designated harbour of refuge and the present east and west piers were built. A curved end was attached to the west pier in 1740, and the extensions were added early in the twentieth century. (RRB) *32*

11. The east pier; this photograph of the 'iron man' crane shows clearly the complexity of the engineering involved in building the pier extensions. (FMS) 33

12. A late 19th century photograph of the harbour from Larpool shows the twist and turns in the channel out to the piers. Both railways are visible on the left, from Pickering and Scarborough, and on the right is the factory where Prussian blue dye was made. When the trees are bare it is still possible to see the permanently blue colour on the cliff face. Behind the headland in the right foreground was Whitehall shipyard. (FMS) 34

13. An eighteenth century print of an early drawbridge. (RRB) 35

14. Sutcliffe's photograph of a print of a later bridge. (FMS) 36

15. This photograph shows the newer of the two bridges over Spital beck. Through the arch can be seen the remains of the 'timber pond' in which masts and large baulks of timber intended for ship-building were stored to prevent them from drying out. (RRB) 37

16. A steamship on the stocks at Turnbull and Scott's shipyard at Whitehall. (FMS) 38

17. Whitby's first harbour tugs were paddle steamers. It is easy to be romantic about steam, but in fact the pollution from the coal-fired boilers must have been considerable. (FMS) 39

18. The great terror of the days of sail was to be close to the land in an 'on-shore' gale, blowing from the sea, in a rising spring tide. This combination of wind, current and geography was called a 'lee-shore'. This brig has been driven aground because the forces were simply too strong for the crew to fight, and even her anchors would have dragged. She might have been refloated, but more likely, if the gale continued, she would have broken up. The crew might well have drowned trying to get ashore, though there would have been many willing hands from the town trying to help them. (FMS) 49

19. Even steamers could come to grief on a lee-shore if their engines failed. This photograph taken near Sandsend shows the hard work involved in trying to preserve the ship in the hope of refloating her, and in the general salvage of anything that could be saved should their efforts fail. (FMS) 50

20. Henry Freeman, wearing the cumbersome cork life-jacket which saved him as the only survivor of the upsetting of the lifeboat in the great storm of 1861. Henry was tall and strong, and could work while wearing the jacket, which was too constraining for his slighter fellow crewmen. The lifeboat memorial in St Mary's church recounts the events of that terrible day. (FMS) 51

21. Saltwick Bay and Black Nab; the shore round the bay has many archaeological remains, of alum works and a medieval harbour; the white streaks on the cliffs are of dissolved alum leaching out of the shale. (FMS)
52

22. Women's work: women and girls gathering flithers or limpets from the rocky shore to be use to bait fishing lines. It was hard, cold work. (FMS)
53

23. The herring fleet setting out under sail. (FMS)
54

24. The 166 ton brig *Opal* at the New Quay, on the edge of the former graving dock. A brig had two masts, both square-rigged. (FMS)
55

25. This shows the two parallel sheds at the Spital Bridge ropewalk, roofed with typical Whitby pantiles. Rope-making for the standing and running rigging for sailing vessels were an important industry in Whitby for centuries. (FMS)
56

26. Sutcliffe photographed this parchment inserted into the parish register during the Commonwealth period, 1653-1660. All parishes were expected to choose an official called, confusingly, the Register, whose duty it was to record all births, marriages and deaths. This list of the chief citizens of Whitby who acted as electors contains many men involved in the growing shipping industry, as well as many who later became Quakers. (FMS)
57

27. This is a photograph by Sutcliffe of a mid 18th century chart of the approaches to Whitby harbour. It shows the dangerous reef know as Whitby Rock, the leading lines from various directions to the official sea-marks, and at the top a silhouette of the shoreline giving the most visible marks. Such charts were sometimes made in response to a threat of war, when it was necessary for the Navy to know where harbours were and how to approach them. (FMS)
65

28. William Scoresby's map: William Scoresby, senior, drew this map to accompany his political pamphlet, published in 1818, suggesting ways of using seamen left without work after the Napoleonic Wars to undertake public works which would give them employment and improve the economic situation of the town. The map rewards study for its innovative and humane ideas. (Whitby Literary and Philosophical Society)
66

29. The rooflines of St Mary's taken from the Abbey plain, showing the faint outline of the original pitched roof on the wall of the tower. This has been replaced by a flatter roof with roof-lights like those of a ship, constructed by men who were ships' carpenters. Also shown is the extension built in 1818 to replace the north transept, and to give work to former seamen and soldiers after the end of the Napoleonic Wars. (RRB)
67

30. Again this shows the graving dock, but more importantly this is a picture of the oldest Whitby vessel to have been photographed. She is the topsail schooner *Alert*, built by George and Nathaniel Langborne in 1802, and photographed by Frank Meadow Sutcliffe in 1888. (FMS)   76

31. This shows a steam tug towing the hull of a newly built steamship out of the harbour for fitting out elsewhere, and shows the decline of the fortunes of the port, as its size made it unable to cope with the demands of modern shipping. (FMS)   77

32. A romantic view of the inter-tidal mud in Whitby's harbour, with two brigs on their mud berths, and a coble passing across the channel in the moonlight. (FMS)   89

33. This view from the west cliff is less well-known than the *Haven Under the Hill* photograph, but makes the smoky nature of the town clear, though those who had to live with the grime must have puzzled over the popularity of smoky views. (FMS)   90

34. Selling the catch in the days before the fish-market building was erected on the quay. (FMS)   91

35. Whitby in the 19th century. A lithograph produced by Newman and Co, seeing the town from the Mount, and the first railway station.   92

36. The interior of St Mary's Church, showing the slender wooden pillars, made from mast timber, and marbled to resemble stone. The famous three-decker pulpit, still in use, can be clearly seen. (FMS)   99

37. The handsome Victorian reredos in St Hilda's Church, built in the 1880s to serve the growing population on the west cliff. (FMS)   100

38. This illustration should be compared with the Sutcliffe photograph (illustration 12), which still shows sailing brigs. In this recent photograph the masts of the replica ship *Grand Turk* can be made out at the left.   102

39. Young people on educational visits make up a good part of the tourism in this historic town.   103

40. Church Street, formerly Kirkgate, still shows vestiges of the original narrow burgage plots in the small shops facing the street. It is very popular with visitors.   104

41. Looking across the marina to the floating dry-dock, in which fishing and pleasure boats are repaired; on the wharf above is Whitby's working ship-yard, with a 'shrink-wrapped newly built trawler being fitted out, and to the left the iron hull for another vessel being constructed. The completed vessels are launched in the harbour by a giant crane which visits the port for the occasion.   105

A NOTE ON WEIGHTS, MEASURES AND MONEY

The weights, measures and monetary values used in this book are the ones contemporaries used. These may be summarised as:

Money:

4 farthings	=	1d (penny)
12d (pence)	=	1s (shilling)
1s	=	5p
20s (shillings)	=	£1 (pound)
21s (shillings)	=	1 guinea

Weight:

16oz (ounces)	=	1lb (pound)
1lb	=	0.45 kilograms
14lb (pounds)	=	1 stone
1 stone	=	6.35 kilograms
2 stones	=	1qr (quarter)
1qr	=	12.70 kilograms
4qr (quarters)	=	1cwt (hundredweight)
1cwt	=	50.80 kilograms
20cwt	=	1 ton
1 ton	=	1.02 tonnes

Volume:

2 pints	=	1 quart
1 quart	=	1.14 litres
4 quarts	=	1 gallon
1 gallon	=	4.55 litres
2 gallons	=	1 peck
1 peck	=	9.09 litres
4 pecks	=	1 bushel
1 bushel	=	36.40 litres
8 bushels	=	1qr (quarter)
1 quarter	=	2.91 hectolitres

Distance:

12in (inches)	=	1ft (foot)
1ft	=	0.305 metres
3ft (feet)	=	1yd (yard)
1yd	=	0.91 metres
22yds (yards)	=	1 chain
1 chain	=	20.12 metres
10 chains	=	1 furlong
1 furlong	=	201.17 metres
8 furlongs	=	1 mile
1 mile	=	1.61 kilometres

Area:

30¼ sq yds	=	1 perch
1 perch	=	25.29 sq metres

40 perches = 1 rood = 1210 sq yds = 1011.56 sq metres
4 roods = 1 acre = 4840 sq yds = 0.405 hectares

Prepared by Stephen Harrison

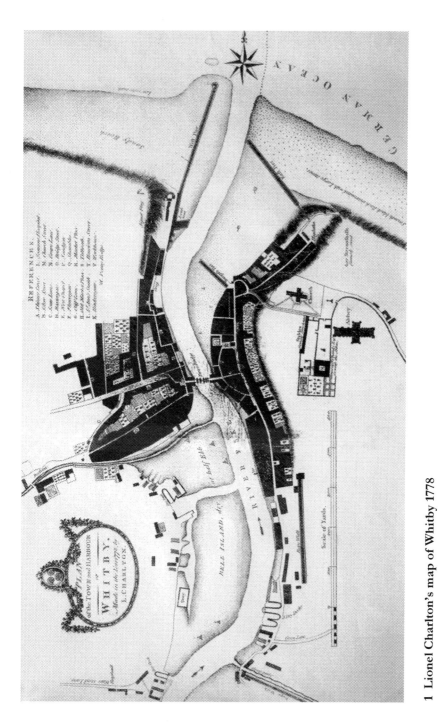

1 Lionel Charlton's map of Whitby 1778

CHAPTER 1

FOUNDATIONS

Whitby has passed through three lives, and is engaged on its fourth. It was a major religious centre before the Norman Conquest; it had a long period of growth during the middle ages as a dependent town of the abbey; after the dissolution of the abbey it gradually developed as a major ship-building and ship-owning port in the age of sail; finally, with the coming of the railway, and the decline of sailing ships, it became a holiday resort. As well as those lives, it has had two names, *Streoneshalh* and *Whitby*, each equally famous, and at all times it has performed on a wide international stage. Yet it is, apparently, a small place, isolated, constrained by geography to be exceeded in size by all its rivals.

Whitby lies at the mouth of the Yorkshire Esk, a river some twenty-four miles in length. The Esk rises as a series of small streams known as the Esklets in the northern part of the North York Moors National Park, on Westerdale Moor, flows initially in a northerly direction, then, at Danby, turns easterly and flows to the sea, turning northerly again in its last mile, to enter the sea through its narrow, north-facing estuary. Whitby is one of the few places on the east coast of England where, in summer, the sun both rises and sets in the sea.

The North York Moors are some 39 miles wide by 22 miles deep, of sedimentary rock, heavily glaciated, and rise to over a thousand feet in the Cleveland Hills in the west. They are wild and desolate in winter, but beautiful, and much favoured by walkers, naturalists and geologists. In the past the moors were a considerable barrier to landward travel, and part of their influence has been to force Whitby to look towards the sea. At the same time they have provided, particularly in the Esk valley, and in the other dales on the north side of the moors, a population which has looked to Whitby as a market town, and as a port for sea travel, while Whitby has in turn considered the moors a source of its river and the melt-water from snow which helped to give the town a precious water supply, as pasture for stock, and as a source of timber, stone and minerals.

The Esk runs into the North Sea between two cliffs, each of which rises to almost 200 feet. These, the east and west cliffs, confuse visitors who are new to the town, for they feel that Whitby, like most other east coast resorts, ought to face east. On the east cliff are the ruins of the abbey, St Mary's Parish Church, the shell of the Cholmley mansion, which houses the visitor centre, and other more recent buildings. From the parish churchyard there is a steep, cobbled lane down to the town, known as the 'donkey road', beside the better-known 199 Church Stairs, for centuries in the care of the churchwardens of the parish.

The oldest part of the town lies on the small area of level land around the lowest bridging point of the Esk, some 48 acres, about half of which is intertidal mud. It is congested by the shortage of building land, though now much more open than in the 19th century. There is a commercial wharf and a fishing port, as well as the inevitable marina. One ship-building slipway remained until recently, but its last task was to provide a site for the manufacture of a floating dry-dock, which provides repair facilities for Whitby's fishing fleet, and for similar-sized vessels from other ports. Beside it, is a small ship-yard which builds modern fishing boats.

Some streets, as well as the narrow yards which lead off the main thoroughfares, climb precipitously up the sides of both cliffs, and the Church Stairs is by no means the only long flight of public steps in Whitby. High on the west cliff are the houses built for the new visitors who arrived in the town after the railway came. The railway from Pickering was designed by George Stephenson, in 1836, and now survives between Grosmont, where it links with Network Rail, and Pickering, as the North York Moors Railway, although the track between Whitby and Grosmont has now been strengthened to take the NYMR's steam trains, which come right through to Whitby in the summer months. On the outskirts of the town are the modern houses which replaced some of the crowded housing of the old town. Whitby once had the dubious distinction of being the most congested central township in the north of England, as the expanding town tried to fit into the limits of the tiny medieval burgage. The population size has changed little over the last century.

Round the cliffs are the spring lines which gave Whitby its water in the past, and which became its spas. They have been a mixed blessing, for they can also cause serious landslips. The cliffs themselves have been much eroded, partially by the sea, and by efforts to extract from them both jet and alum, but also from the action of the 'perched', or high,

2

water-table, sliding over impermeable clay, and taking considerable chunks of cliff with it. The last major fall took place in January 2005.

The Esk provides the only safe natural estuarine harbour on the hundred mile long coast between Tees and Humber, and has probably been settled since the New Stone Age at least. There are artefacts in Whitby Museum which cover a long period of occupation. There are stone axes, saws and knives, as well as beads of the jet for which Whitby much later became famous. Apart from good examples of cup and ring-marked stones found in the area around Whitby, there are bronze implements, including an elaborate socketed dagger, parts of swords, and more domestic implements. A devastating fire which destroyed almost 1,000 acres of moor in 2003 has revealed a wealth of archaeological artefacts from the stone age to World War 2. The Romans came, to a region which belonged to the *Brigantes*, and left their mark behind, in the site of a Roman signal station at Goldsborough, probably linked to the stretch of Roman Road which lies exposed on Wheeldale Moor, and which may have stretched from Malton to Goldsborough. There is good evidence from the Roman period, and Whitby Museum has fine examples discovered in both the town and the district, including jet mined from the cliffs.

The best-known part of Whitby's history, however, begins after the Roman armies were recalled to the defence of Rome, around 410AD, leaving the Romano-British inhabitants of 'Britannia' to defend themselves. These were probably of mixed Celtic and Belgic origin, and by the beginning of the fifth century, when Rome was threatened by the barbarians, Christianised. They have left behind them the name of their river, the Esk. The peoples of northern Germany, the Angles, Saxons and Jutes recorded in Bede's *History of the English Church and People*, themselves under pressure from barbarians, and from shortage of land, moved over the North Sea to settle, and it is with them that this history begins, not in *Whitby* but in the older *Streoneshalh*, which found early fame throughout Western Europe in the 7th century.

The meaning of the name *Streoneshalh* is controversial; various experts have produced theories, all of which agree that the second part of the name is topographical, and suggests a sheltered, enclosed or reclaimed place. *Streon* could be a personal name, or it could mean 'a descent', or even 'reclaimed land'. There is no contemporary documentary evidence to link Whitby with the older settlement, but there is archaeological evidence of a major Anglo-Saxon site, and too much circumstantial evidence and later documentation for there to be more than a lingering doubt in a few academic circles. Major archaeological investigations carried out by English Heritage during the building of their state-of-the-art visitor centre, revealed a hitherto unsuspected major, high-status Anglo-Saxon town, with evidence of glass- and metal-working, and of intellectual activity. The final report is eagerly awaited. A range of the most recent finds is on display in the visitor centre.

The settlers in this part of North Yorkshire were Angles, probably either from the southern part of Denmark or from the coastal strip of northeast Germany. They founded two kingdoms, Deira and Bernicia, which were later united to become Northumbria. There are place-names in the district which hark back to the earliest Anglian settlements, with Old English elements in the name. *Fyling* is an early name, found in Fylingthorpe and Fylingdale, though amalgamated with later Norse words. The earliest recorded history of the settlement at *Streoneshalh* is to be found in Bede's *History*. Bede wrote in the 8th century, in his monastery at Jarrow in County Durham, and used earlier sources which have not survived. He recounted the development of the English nation, and the growth of the Church within it, for the new settlers were pagan, though they came to a Christian country. Bede chronicled the conversion of the kingdom of Northumbria, through the coming of St Paulinus from Kent in the train of the Kentish Princess Ethelburga who was to marry King Edwin. In due course Edwin was himself baptised, together with his kin, among whom was his thirteen-year-old great-niece, the orphaned Hild, named with the Anglo-Saxon word for 'struggle', born a prisoner of war in Elmet after her father's death in battle.

It was Hild, or Hilda, to use the more common Latin form, who came to the King's town at *Streoneshalh* in 657 to carry out the vow of King Oswy, Edwin's nephew, that a monastery would be founded there in thanksgiving for the defeat of Penda, the still heathen King of Mercia. When Oswy called her to this mission, Hilda was already Abbess of the abbey at Hartlepool, and, despite her conversion by Paulinus, who came from the Roman tradition, was much influenced by Aidan, one of the missionaries of the Celtic church, which derived in part from the original Romano-British church, and in part from Columba and the monks of Iona. The basic beliefs were the same as those of Rome, but the practice of the Celtic church varied in some respects, because it had been for long isolated from the influence of Rome. The method of calculating Easter was different, and so were the monastic practices.

The monastery which Hilda founded was in the Celtic form, a double house for men and women, though they were entirely separated. It

4

says much for the Anglo-Saxon view of women that most of these double houses were ruled by women such as Hilda, scholarly, good organisers, respected throughout Christendom as teachers and trainers of men.

It was to Hilda's monastery that in 664, the princes of the English church and state came to debate whether the English church, now well established in faith, should follow the Celtic practice or the practice of Rome. Hilda was in favour of the Celtic rite, but when King Oswy, presiding in an abbey dedicated to St Peter, cast his vote for Rome, on the grounds that, as Bede wryly reports, St Peter carried the keys to Heaven, Hilda accepted the judgment.

Hilda is remembered today for this Synod of Whitby, but in her own time she was famous as an educator of men for the high office of the Church. Among the men and women who were professed and trained at *Streoneshalh* were Saints John of Beverley, Wilfrid and Bosa, all of whom became Bishops of York, as well as her own successor, Ælfleda, and Cædmon. Cædmon was never a prince of the Church, unlike Whitby's other saints. He was first recorded by Bede, as a herdsman of some kind working around the abbey. His name suggests that he may have been of British rather than Anglian stock. According to Bede, the lay servants were wont to meet in the evening for singing, but Cædmon was inclined to slip away, since extempore song was not his skill.

One night, Bede recorded, Cædmon retired to his bed, and there had a vision in which an angel bade him sing of the 'beginning of created things'. He composed a song, one of the earliest known surviving pieces of 'English' poetry. In the morning he told what had happened to him, and was taken before the Abbess. She was said to have set him searching tasks to prove the truth of what he said, and when he had convinced her, she took him into the monastery, where he lived out his life as a monk, writing sacred poetry based on the Bible. Though much Anglo-Saxon poetry remains, some of it attributed to Cædmon, it is not possible to say accurately if any more of his work has actually survived. In 1902 a cross in the style of his own time was erected at the top of the Church Stairs in memory of this gentle man.

Hilda died in 680, and her death is recorded with honour in both Bede's *History* and the *Anglo-Saxon Chronicle*. It is not known whether her remains still lie in the grounds. It was for a long time said that the monks fled from Danish invasions, taking the body of their beloved foundress with them, but the recent archaeological evidence shows no evidence of the destruction long thought to have happened to Hilda's abbey in the 9th century. It was at Hilda's abbey that the earliest known *Life of St Gregory the*

Great was written, by an unknown monk, recording the decision to send missionaries to convert the heathen Anglo-Saxons. The same text records the 'miraculous finding of King Edwin's bones where he had been buried after his death in the battle of Hatfield Chase, and their burial at Whitby'.

The destruction of many other Christian sites in Northumbria, including Lindisfarne and York, and the foundation of a Danish kingdom based on York in 876, probably forced the influence of *Streoneshalh* into a decline, as Northumbria ceased to be the dominant Anglo-Saxon kingdom, and there followed a long period for which there is only place-name evidence, notoriously unreliable. *Streoneshalh* became, at some time during the next two hundred years, but probably in the 10th century, *Whitby*, probably the 'white' or stone 'settlement', although another school of thought suggests that *Hviti* may have been a personal name. It is now thought from its earliest recorded forms not to be Danish, but a name given by later Norwegian settlers, who came over the North Sea to join their kin migrating from earlier settlements on the west coast. Whether they were Christian by the time they arrived is not known, but they gave the name *Prestibi*, the 'farm of the priests', to a settlement in or around Whitby, possibly even to the site of the abbey itself, and it was still there at the time of the *Domesday Book*, in 1086. This argues some kind of religious community, but no real trace of it has so far been found.

The years between the destruction of the Northumbrian abbey and the coming of King William the Conqueror are recounted in that unique vernacular record, the *Anglo-Saxon Chronicle*. The whole of north-east England came under that vast area of land known as the Danelaw, though many of the settlers were actually Norwegian rather than Danish. The area around Whitby became part of the *Wapentake* of Langbaurgh, and the North Riding or *Thriding* of Yorkshire. Times were often unsettled, and from the *Chronicle* it is easy to imagine that these were centuries of constant turmoil, but there would be long periods when individual communities, though they might need to be watchful, would carry on with daily life in peace. The comparative survey given in the *Domesday Book* shows that Whitby, which had belonged to Siward, Earl of Northumbria, till his death in 1055, had been worth £112 per annum. Most of the place-names in and around Whitby itself seem to be Norwegian, like Larpool and Stakesby, but that there were Danish settlements is shown by the parish of Danby, the *village of the Danes*. Siward himself was a Dane, who became Earl during the time of King Cnut.

The next watershed in history came in 1066. To a kingdom with an ordered and fairly sophisticated way of life, with sound laws and a functional form of local government, came Duke William of Normandy. King Harold Godwinson had been dealing with a northern rebellion, which ended in the battle of Stamford Bridge, about 40 miles south-west of Whitby, and was forced to march south at speed. William defeated the English at Hastings, and became King of England. The northern English were reluctant to submit to William, and risings between 1067 and 1069 brought devastating retribution from the Normans. In the episode known as the *Harrying of the North*, King William laid waste his northern territory.

So much was destroyed that when the *Domesday* commissioners came sixteen years later, in the northern counties there was little to survey, since most of the land was still waste. A few places escaped, and church land was spared, but the general economic base of the region had been destroyed, so that little of the wealth of what the *Domesday Book* calls the *Time of King Edward* survived. Siward's holding at Whitby, by then in the hands of Hugh, Earl of Chester, and his sub-tenant William de Percy, was worth a mere 60 shillings; because part of it was in church hands it had been spared it the worst, but its decline had been drastic. Whenever there is a serious moor fire in the area, it is possible to imagine what effect the *harrying* had on huge tracts of land. Often nothing grows for years after the fire; wild animals and grazing livestock are killed, and in any case their fodder has been destroyed. The entire viable agricultural land of the north of England would have gone.

Yet out of the *Harrying of the North* came Whitby's second period of importance, because, as recounted in the *Abbot's Book*, the Whitby Cartulary, Reinfrid, a soldier in King William's service, who had been greatly distressed by the ruins of the northern abbeys destroyed by the Danes, became professed as a monk at Evesham, and, with two others, sought permission to travel north to refound some of the monasteries. After some wanderings, he came to Whitby, where William de Percy granted him land, much of which had probably been land attached to St Hilda's abbey, and thus the great Benedictine house of St Peter and St Hilda was founded, with Reinfrid as its first Prior.

2 Part of the east pier and the east headland looking up to St Mary's church and the Abbey ruins.

3 The Spa ladder

4 The 199 Church Stairs, which lead from Henrietta Street to St Mary's churchyard.

CHAPTER 2

NORMAN ABBEY AND MEDIEVAL TOWN

One of the most useful records of any monastic house is its *Cartulary*, the book in which the monastery recorded the grants of land, bequests, charters and other important entitlements which it possessed. The *Cartulary* of Whitby Abbey, based on the surviving *Great Book of Whitby* or *Abbot's Book* in Whitby Museum, and other manuscripts, was published by the Surtees Society in two volumes, in the original Latin and Norman-French. It has recently been translated into English through the auspices of the *Friends of Whitby Abbey*, to make it much more accessible to a modern audience.

Early charters seem to indicate that Reinfrid's son, Fulco or Fulke, was *dapifer*, or steward, to William de Percy, the principal benefactor of the refounded abbey. Fulco, whose own local holding is recorded in the *Domesday Book*, gave land to the abbey, so there was a family element in the refounding. William's brother, Serlo, is recorded as having succeeded Reinfrid as Prior when Reinfrid was killed. The story of Reinfrid's death gives us an endearing picture of the man, for he is described as having come across a bridge-building party at Ormesbridge, near Hackness, a daughter house, on his return on horseback from a journey. He dismounted and rushed unwisely in to help, and was killed by a falling beam. The affection in which he was held is shown by the use of the diminutive *corpusculum*, his 'little body', in the description of his carrying to Hackness for burial.

Hugh, Earl of Chester, had been granted the Whitby lands by his uncle, William the Conqueror. William de Percy was also a tenant-in-chief in his own right, holding land directly from the King, and it was from his *chief* holding that he gave Hackness to the new monastery. Percy himself died in Palestine on the First Crusade. Hugh, after a somewhat dissolute life, became a monk before his death. However these warrior barons had conducted themselves in the prime of their lives, they were deeply aware of the importance of religious faith. The military nature of those who founded and endowed the great abbeys reflects the ethos behind the feudal system, that it was concerned with the provision of knight service to the king, and even more that the conquest of England was an élite affair, by comparatively few, but very militaristic, barons and knights. Even Odo, Bishop of Bayeux, the Conqueror's half-brother, appears in his own Bayeux Tapestry as a warrior, rather than as an ecclesiastic.

The history of the very early years of the new monastery is somewhat confused. There are various versions of their struggles, but what emerges as the most likely is that from time to time the monks were beset by pirates and other raiders, as well as by personality clashes amongst themselves and with their founder. Certainly at one time they withdrew to Hackness for a while, and in about 1086 a group of monks, probably under Stephen, a strong-minded man, left to refound Lastingham, the former Priory of St Cedd, but finding it very remote, moved again to York, to found St Mary's Abbey, of which Stephen was the first abbot. It was in turn from York that a later group of monks left to join the stricter Cistercian Order and establish Fountains Abbey, among them being Robert, who was professed at Whitby, and who became eventually St Robert of Newminster. In the later abbey as well as in the first, saints were nurtured in Whitby. Some may even have ended their days at the tiny Priory of Rumburgh in east Suffolk, where there was a daughter house of St Mary's Abbey in York, a strangely four-square building amongst the delicate narrow flint towers of its Suffolk neighbours.

Until 1086-7 the monastery at Whitby was a Priory, and administratively the land was part of the Wapentake of Langbaurgh, but about that time, Serlo either retired or was deposed, and William de Percy, a nephew of the founder, replaced him, at the same time becoming abbot, so that the monastery, within ten years of its foundation, had become a major abbey. Its land became a liberty, separated from the Wapentake, and with considerable privileges. These grants were confirmed by King William II, and gave Whitby an important place in the history of medieval England. It meant that in due course Abbots would be invited to attend Parliament, would be deputed to undertake important tasks on behalf of the King, and would host meetings of the Benedictine Houses of the Northern Province, and that the abbey would be recognised as a place of pilgrimage. It brought Whitby into the national context, so that much of Whitby's history can be traced not only in the cartulary and other local documents, but also in State, Crown, and Papal archives for several hundred years.

The abbey prospered, given lands by a widening circle of benefactors, both in England and in Scotland, some of it so far away that administration must have been difficult, to the point where it would be leased in later times to other religious houses. The dissolution documents show that some endowments were given jointly to both Whitby and Meaux, near Hull. The good intentions expressed on deathbeds were not always practical. Sometimes such endowments led to acrimonious lawsuits, when heirs objected to land being alienated to the Church, and sometimes there were disagreements between Religious, such as the Abbot of Whitby and the Bishop of Carlisle, over the possession of land or of tithes and other kinds of income. Among the most important endowments was the grant by Peter de Brus which led to the foundation of a cell at Middlesbrough, which then became part of the liberty. That the industrial sprawl of Middlesbrough should once have been a dependant of the much smaller port of Whitby is now ironic. King Robert I of Scotland, better known as Robert the Bruce, or de Brus of Annandale, was a descendant of Peter, whose *caput* or headquarters was at Danby Castle in Eskdale.

Of all the abbey ruins in England, Whitby is the most easily recognised and most prominent. It stands high on the east cliff, a sea-mark with an immense horizon, which probably saved it from the worse destruction which befell so many abbey churches in the sixteenth century. It is orientated more or less east-west, and built of warm Aislaby stone, whose colours range from silver-grey to chocolate brown. The familiar eastern wall of the choir and presbytery standing above the abbey pond is one of the most photographed constructions in Britain.

The abbey chronicler explained, long after Reinfrid's death, that when Reinfrid came, there were many visible signs of the ruins of St Hilda's abbey. These are now buried, but there have been excavations at various times during this century, most recently in conjunction with the construction of the new visitor centre in Cholmley House, during the late 1990s. The Norman monks did not rebuild the Northumbrian abbey. They began again, and first built a church in the Norman style, whose outline can be seen within the present ruins. It was the early 12th century which produced, under Abbot Roger de Scarborough, the choir and presbytery in the Early English style. It is known, however, that the task set by Abbot Roger sent the abbey deeply into debt by the middle of the 13th century, and again by 1320.

Building continued throughout the abbey's history, though most of what is visible today was completed by the 15th century. The abbey church had a fine tower, which stood until 25th June, 1820, and then fell down. Other parts had fallen long before, some of them during the lifetime of the monastery. Gaskin refers to an account of a tremendous storm of wind and snow about Martinmas (10th November) 1334, during which the newly completed work on the fabric of the south side of the nave was blown to the ground. It was rebuilt, but at a cost. The last serious collapse was in 1914, when the bombardment of Whitby by a German flotilla damaged the west end of the ruins.

The domestic buildings lay on the south side of the abbey and recent excavation suggests that they had absorbed a good deal of the building 'budget'. However, Benedictine abbeys did not have the large population of monks and lay-brothers that would have been found in a Cistercian abbey, but although these buildings might have been smaller in size than those of Rievaulx, they would still be substantial, and would include guest-houses, abbot's lodgings, infirmary, refectory and dormitories. From afar the abbey would have resembled a small town.

The abbey church itself was dedicated to Ss Peter and Hilda, but within it were altars to other saints, and these are recorded in wills, and in the only surviving parts of the abbey accounts. Even as late as 1540, after the dissolution, John Conyers asked to be buried in front of the altar to St Katherine. Pilgrims came to the abbey to honour and pray to the saints associated with Whitby, and the prosperity the pilgrims brought, and their demands for souvenirs, may well have provided much of the income of Walter the Goldsmith who paid his subsidy, or tax, in 1301. It is likely that King Henry III spent part of the Christmas season of 1251 in Whitby, for his wine-buyer, Robert de Dacre, was instructed to arrange for 10 tuns of wine to be sent to Whitby, and 100 tuns to York, for the King's Christmas celebrations. Walter de Gray, Archbishop of York, had been the King's tutor in his minority, after the death of King John, Henry's father, in 1216. As a tun held 252 gallons, the festivities were probably quite cheerful.

Nowadays the abbey church is a spectacular ruin, but for centuries the complex was a home for the monks who served in it, and a focal point for the people of a liberty some sixty miles in circumference. For these people a parish church was provided. *Domesday* has no record of a church in Whitby, though three were recorded in the Percy holdings at Hackness with Suffield and Everley. There would have been a church associated with St Hilda's abbey, even if it had fallen into disuse. The Norse name *Prestibi* in *Domesday* suggests that priests may still have been there, and must have had a building for worship.

However, the present parish church, St Mary's, was begun in about 1110. It is nearer to the present town than is the abbey, at the head of what became the 199 Church Stairs. It is frequently mentioned in the records of both the abbey and the town, and like the abbey church, though for different reasons, it is one of the most visited parish churches in England.

When the abbey was refounded there was a *vill* at Whitby, mentioned in the earliest charters, together with a port. Its size is unknown, but its site was important because of the estuary, which afforded shelter from storms for the inexact, coast-watching navigation of early times. The river itself was only navigable for a short length, but it provided abundant fast-flowing water, necessary for health both as drinking water, and as a means of carrying away the waste of the townsfolk. In the early modern period, when parish records are systematic, it becomes clear that something, probably abundance of water, and the steep slopes which would carry waste to the fast flowing estuary, protected Whitby's population from many of the usual health hazards which the growing congestion of the town might have produced.

With the foundation charters came the right to hold a market, but in the 1120s the growing community was recognised in the grant of *burgage* by Henry I to the Abbot. This was the foundation of Whitby as a borough, still subservient to the Abbot, but with distinct trade and craft opportunities. When a Norman town was 'planted', so-called *burgage plots* were made available, with frontages, usually narrow, around 15 feet, on to the principal thoroughfares of the town. These became the shop-fronts for the businesses carried on within the buildings, and the craftsman or merchant and his family lived on the premises. Such plots might be available for money rent or for some services on the manor, as with any other manorial holding.

The streets on to which the burgages fronted would be wide enough for wheeled vehicles, and would be linked by narrow passage-ways suitable for porters, or for hand-barrows. Burgage plots were long and narrow, with garths to the rear for growing food and providing 'keep' for livestock. An infrastructure providing food from the hinterland would have been slow to develop. These garths were later filled in with smaller dwellings as pressure on land increased in growing towns. The extent of the burgage would be defined in early documents no longer extant, and the status of a holding within that defined area, both for trade and for security reasons, kept expansion within its limits. *Sub*urban meant below the town, beneath its dignity, until recent times.

During the Abbacy of Richard, in the 1180s, the *Burgesses* were granted *free burgage*, a great privilege, which gave them freedom from tolls on the main thoroughfares, freedom from customs dues, and freedom from manorial duties. The burgesses were entitled to hold courts three times a year. It was a recognition by a generous abbot of the growing importance of the town. The charter was confirmed by King John, in the first year of his reign, but alas Abbot Richard had died, and his successor, Peter, was dismayed to discover how much of the abbey's income in tolls and dues had been alienated to the town, so he petitioned John to have the burgage charter rescinded. The burgesses counter-petitioned, but John decided in favour of the Abbot, and the independence was lost. From time to time over the next 150 years the burgesses, who had retained vestigial powers, tried to have the decision reversed, but failed. Long after the dissolution the burgesses petitioned King Charles I in 1630/31 for the right to have a Recorder, and to become an incorporated borough. The King viewed the request favourably, and ordered Letters Patent to be issued, but nothing came of them, for reasons unknown. Perhaps the probable cost of the charter offended their Yorkshire thriftiness.

The first grant of burgage had confirmed market rights, and the market was held on the Lord's Day until 1425-6, when King Henry VI forbade the holding of a market on Sunday, so that Saturday became market-day. A fair had also been granted, to be held on 25th August, the Feast of the Translation of St Hilda, and after the Reformation that expanded to three days, beginning on 24th August, St Bartholomew's day. A second fair, held around 17th November, St Hilda's day proper, developed by 'custom'. Fairs around Martinmas, November the 10th, were common, and suited the economic year in a pastoral and seafaring society, coming after the great sheep sales, and at the end of the normal sailing season in the stormy North Sea, when men were available for hire, and had money in their pockets to spend.

There are several factors which distinguish towns from villages, and Whitby shows most of them. It provided a market accessible to a large hinterland, mainly within the liberty of the abbey, but also to the population which lived to the west, on the lands of Mulgrave Castle, and to those who lived in the royal Forest of Pickering. It had a wider catchment area because of the port, and as early as the 12th century was frequented by Flemish and Italian merchants in search of wool and of salt fish. It was strategically placed in its proximity, a variable distance because of border conflicts in the middle ages, to Scotland, and was at times required to furnish ships against the Scots. In 1451 the royal French bastard, d'Orleans, and his retainers, in nine French ships, were captured and brought into Whitby. This must have provided an exotic interlude, and a good deal of trade, for the inhabitants of the town, although they would have no share in any ransom money.

Although there was never the wide range of merchant and craft guilds found in larger provincial centres, at least three guilds dedicated to religious purposes and mutual support did exist, those of Holy Trinity, Holy Cross and, appropriately for a growing port, St Christopher. Whitby merchants became members of guilds in other towns, such as the Guild of Corpus Christi in York. The archives of the Merchant Adventurers of York record in 1368 a feast held for their Whitby members.

The surnames given in the Lay Subsidy of 1301, at a time when the use of surnames was still fluid, show a range of occupational names; these include cobbler, baker, weaver, toll-gatherer, barber, pier-master, fell-monger, skinner, dyer, stonemason and goldsmith. This was a very stringent taxation, levied at a rate of 1/15th, a low level which ensured that even the poor were assessed, though in Whitby no-one paid less than 6½d, whereas in other places amounts as low as 2d were paid. What the taxation lists, published by the Yorkshire Archaeological Society, show is that Whitby and its liberty were the third wealthiest places after York and the liberty of St Mary's Abbey.

Customs accounts from the early 14th century show that Whitby's principal trade was in herrings, and that the port was frequented by merchants from Lombardy, and from most of the North Sea ports of Europe. Merchants came from all over England, even from Wales and Cheshire, but mostly from the east coast. This is borne out by the placenames which began to appear as surnames in 1301, including the Scottish port of Mussleburgh. These were not just visitors, but people with an economic stake in the town. One of them, Peter de Lincoln, described as 'of Whitby', was in 1321 granted his first recorded safe-conduct by King Edward II to go over the seas to trade. His adventures included being captured by pirates off the coast of Sussex, and living to tell the tale, in 1327.

By the end of the 14th century, the abbey's only surviving set of accounts show that Whitby had already embarked on the coal trade which was to be its standby for centuries. The Crown granted to the Abbot the right to collect tolls for the maintenance of quays, as in 1306/7; the maintenance of the quay was a constant problem, and in 1341 the sea broke the quay up. To the Burgesses were granted similar tolls for the upkeep of the bridge. Whitby wills include bequests for the bridge, for such a bequest was considered a pious act. The tollbooth was on the east side, where the present market is held, and near the old Shambles. It was rebuilt at various times, and the present building was erected in 1788.

Whitby, like any other town, had problems of poverty and disability. Not everyone could work, even in a growing urban community. There were many bequests to the abbey for the relief of poverty, and there was a leper hospital, whose first patient, Orm, is the earliest 'patient' known by name in England. By 1320 there was a second hospital, of St John the Baptist. When these were dissolved along with the abbey, there would be nothing to take their place, nor would there be provision for the relief of poverty, except for such private charity which might come from individuals.

By the time of the dissolution of the abbey, Whitby, although still only a manorial borough, would be visibly a town, flourishing, becoming congested, and with a busy harbour. The abbey still had at least 24 monks, and current research shows that the complement may have been much more. Although most of its land was leased out, it was scattered over a large part of north-east England. Its annual income, net of dues, was about £437, less than that of other great Benedictine abbeys, but still large. Its last years were quarrelsome, with the bailiff, Gregory Conyers, with the townsfolk, who rioted when prevented from holding what they considered to be a customary procession, and with the King who suspected involvement with the Pilgrimage of Grace.

The monks acquired a new abbot, Henry Divall, almost at the end, and managed to avoid impeachment, a fate which befell other Northern houses. There were querulous letters from the abbot to Cardinal Wolsey, and then, after a visitation, the monks were forced to surrender, on December 14th, 1539. The roof was stripped, the bells removed, and the valuables taken away. The monks were pensioned off, and went their ways, some to become parish priests. The domestic buildings were quarried for stone. The abbey church survived as well as it might without a protected roof, because it was an important seamark. A legend mentioned by the 18th century historian, Lionel Charlton, said that the ship carrying the bells sank off Saltwick Nab, and that they can still be heard. The land was eventually bought by the Cholmleys, who had leased it from about 1541, and their much altered house stands beside the abbey. The great Tudor topographer, John Leland, visited Whitby, and his description published in 1540 described it as a '*great* fischar toun' (my italics). He recounted that its harbour was protected by a pier and that the quay was being rebuilt with stones fallen from the cliff. However, he must have visited it before the dissolution, because within a year the chief citizens of the town were replying to a request for naval support for King Henry VIII, with a lamentable tale of collapse and poverty.

It is clear from such evidence as has survived that during the remaining years of the century Whitby had become a shadow of the wealthy abbey town of the high middle ages. There seems to have been little shipping, and minimal use of its harbour for trade. It was a fishing port, but there is no evidence of the normal trading activity of a town. It was not just that the poor would have missed their alms; it was that the considerable income of the abbey, which would have been spent in Whitby, had gone. So too had the pilgrims and other important visitors to the abbey. There was no goldsmith now.

5 Rumburgh Priory

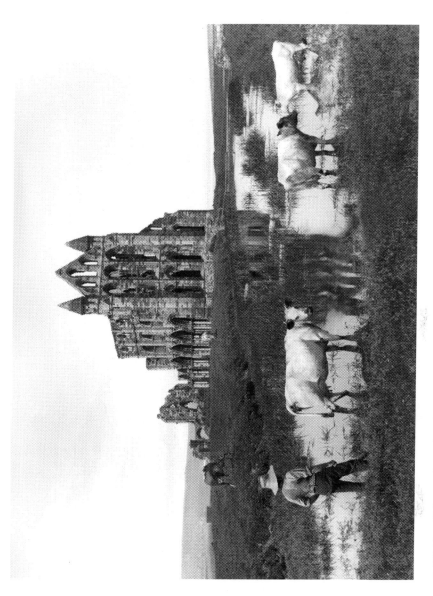

6 Whitby Abbey ruins, showing the Early English east end, with the mediaeval Abbey pond

7 Market day, on the present market site

8 Argument's Yard, 'Argument' being a local surname.

CHAPTER 3

THE RIVER ESK

The topographer Richard Blome, writing in 1673, described Whitby as being 'commodiously setted upon the River Esk at its influx into the sea', and in 1675 the great mapmaker John Ogilby described the Esk as one of the principal rivers of the County of York, while Daniel Defoe, in about 1720, described it as a 'little nameless river, scarce indeed worth a name'. Yet the reason for his comment lies in his astonishment at the size of Whitby's fleet, and at the town's great wealth, despite its apparently 'negligible' river. Most wealthy ports of such importance lay on great rivers such as Thames, Humber or Tyne, with important agricultural hinterlands and often considerable mineral resources.

The Esk is not a long river, but it is a salmon river. Its length is about 24 miles from its source in Westerdale, and for most of its length it is narrow, rocky and fast-flowing, but it has served Whitby well for many centuries. Indeed the town's water supply is still drawn from it. Only the last reach is navigable, from Ruswarp weir to the harbour entrance, and the upper part only for small vessels such as fishing cobles. Spital Bridge was the earliest defined limit upstream of the Customs Port of Whitby, though that limit was moved further upstream to Ruswarp in 1724.

The river has cut Whitby town in two from its earliest foundation, and has also been a major thoroughfare for goods and people since the middle ages. The medieval streets follow to some extent its curve, and from these streets 'ghauts' or 'goats', variously spelt in old documents, but in reality narrow alleyways, ran straight to the water's edge, so that goods could be transported across the river in small boats. Tolls were payable on the bridge, so that it was probably cheaper to use river boats for anything bulky or heavy, especially as the network of ghauts ensured almost door to door transport for the streets adjoining the river. The accounts for the building of the new chapel in Baxtergate in 1778 show payments to boatmen for transporting timber from one ghaut to another.

The earliest recorded bridge is found in the early 14th century, with grants to the burgesses to demand tolls for the upkeep of a bridge.

What kind of bridge is not known, but certainly there were shops, probably booths rather than permanent structures, on the ends of the medieval bridge, for a will of 1541 refers to rents for shops on the bridge. The town was built for trade, and a bridge provided a good opportunity for gathering passing-trade, especially as it was the only dry way across the river. The 18th century drawbridge which appeared in prints was rebuilt in 1766, and replaced in 1835 by a swivel bridge, designed by the harbour engineer, Francis Pickernell, (1796-1871), and in 1908 by an electrically operated swing bridge with a 70 ft wide passageway for shipping. Only in the 1970s was a high level bridge finally built over the Esk above the shipyard. Before that traffic which wanted to avoid the town centre had to go by Ruswarp Bridge.

As well as the bridge there would be fords from the earliest times, variously dangerous as the river rose and fell. The Esk is very susceptible to flooding from its high catchment area, especially after heavy rain, and after thaw, when meltwater rushes fast downstream. Sleights bridge was washed away in 1930 in a flood. A combination of flood-water and spring tides or storms frequently flooded the cellars in the old town, and indeed led to the recurrent need to rebuild the quays. Tidal surges still catch the old town out, and flood the harbour area.

It is difficult to determine the most important aspect of the river in the development of the town. Certainly its importance as a relatively safe haven on the long stretch from Tees to Humber is paramount. That safety probably contributed to its development as a port early in its mercantile history, as did the availability of the cargoes of wool from the abbey lands and above all the herrings which were the staple of its medieval trade. There were ships owned in Whitby from the middle ages, and whenever the Crown required ships then the round-robin letters to the 30 or so principal ports of England generally included Whitby.

Eight ship-builders are recorded in various sources during the 17th century. Phineas Pett, the king's Master Ship-builder, visited one of them, Christopher Bagwith, in 1636. Even earlier the *Great Neptune*, at 500 tons and 40 guns the largest merchant ship in England at the time, was built in Whitby in 1625-6 for the Company of New England. When they failed to pay the bill, Andrew Dickson, the builder, sued at the Privy Council, having presumably sued unsuccessfully in local courts. *Great Neptune* was bought into the Navy, and Andrew Dickson was paid.

During the late 17th and 18th centuries yards proliferated on the Esk, until by 1792 Whitby was high in the list of ship-building towns, and twice reached second place. Given the narrowness of the estuary compared with rivers such as the Tyne and the Thames, that was an extraordinary achievement. The mudflats of Bell Island and the banks on both sides of the river above the bridge were shown in early maps with ships on stocks. There were attendant trades of sail-making, and ropemaking, with rope-walks capable of twisting ropes for the largest ships along the side of the east cliff, one of which is still commemorated in a street name. The great capstans which still stand on the west pier for hauling sailing ships into and out of the harbour give testimony to the strength of these ropes, and to the heavy labour of the men who worked them.

In the 17th century the Netherlands had a very large merchant fleet, but the Navigation Ordinances and Acts of 1650, 1651 and 1660 gave English shipping a monopoly of the growing colonial trade, and the English merchant fleet expanded to meet the demand for English 'bottoms'. When John Haggas, stonemason, died in 1637, he left 5/16ths of one small ship or 'hoy' called the *Welcome* of Whitby to his orphaned seven-year-old grandson, Jonas Haggas. When Jonas died in 1689 he owned shares in ten ships, some of them very large, and was a very wealthy man indeed. He was described in his will as a 'Master and Mariner', and this was a pattern in Whitby, that masters would own shares in a range of ships apart from the one which they commanded. Other probate inventories of the period show that there was a growing fleet of widely ranging sizes of vessel at Whitby.

One of the best known of the shipbuilders of the 18th century was Thomas Fishburn, whose yard built the *Earl of Pembroke* which became the *Endeavour* in which James Cook, Whitby-trained, made his first voyage of discovery. The Fishburn and Brodrick yard flourished for many years, with a good reputation, and the Navy bought or leased other Fishburn ships. One of the ships in the First Fleet, which took the first cargo of convicts and settlers to Botany Bay in 1787-8, was actually named *Fishburn*, and another storeship of that fleet, *Golden Grove*, was also Whitby-built. The logs recounting their voyage out, and their long voyage back round Cape Horn, 'in company', show the qualities of endurance of these sturdy vessels.

There were other shipyards, though, equally competent, and respected, owned by Langbornes, Barrys, Barricks, Campions, Turnbulls, Holts and Richardsons, Chapmans, Wakes and Smales, and there were builders of smaller ships, sloops, schooners and luggers, and of boats. There were mast- and spar-makers, such as Isaac Allanson, block-makers such as John Huntrodes, sail-makers, ropers, chandlers, victuallers, ironmongers, brass-fitters, insurers, cargo agents, dockworkers, seamen, mariners, boatmen. There were flax-dressers, and in the House of Correction, oakum pickers, who unravelled old tarred rope to be used for caulking the seams of the wooden decks and hulls. The banks of the Esk would be the busiest of all thoroughfares in the town, and many of the most important of the 17th century houses had direct access to the river. The house in Grape Lane known as Greengates, once Whitby's first bank, but a typical 18th century town house, with much older parts, has its own wharf at the river side, as has the nearby house in which lived John Walker, the Quaker ship-owner to whom Cook was apprenticed.

But as well as building ships on the river, Whitby used them; to fish, everything from the herrings so sought after both in the middle ages and the early 20th century to the Greenland whales, and to carry cargoes. As she had carried wool from the abbey, so Whitby sent her ships out to the coal trade from the 14th century onwards. And they carried the raw materials and finished product from the 17th and 18th century alum trade, and provided one fifth of all the shipping which brought vital timber, hemp, flax and tar from the Baltic ports to the ship-builders of Whitby and other ports, but particularly to the naval shipyards on the Thames. The Gulf of Riga froze in winter, so that many of these vessels were wintered in the Tyne or the Thames, to ensure a quick start to the next year's trade. However, if major repairs were required they returned to Whitby, adding ship-repair to the uses of the river. The river fed the timber ponds, in which floated the masts and spars, and the baulks of timber awaiting demand. Early maps show William Barker's timber pond, near the main yards. He was one of the principal timber merchants of the town.

However, Whitby remained a small town, and its own consumer needs could have been met by a few small vessels. The large fleet on which Defoe commented, was a service fleet, carrying goods from one major port to another. From the second quarter of the 18th century, it is probable that many Whitby vessels visited their home port only occasionally. The fleet's modern equivalent would probably be the well-known fleets of container lorries which are a familiar sight on British roads.

Even when steam succeeded sail, the Esk was a ship-building port, not only of a continuing line of smaller fishing boats, but of steamers, built at Whitehall shipyard in the 19th and 20th centuries by Turnbull and Scott, of up to 5,700 tons. That was about the limit, and such vessels could not use the port when laden. Its present limit is about 2,000 tons, for vessels which occasionally use the mud berths of the two wharves on the Esk, and for the fishing fleet. The maximum draught is 16 ft at spring tide at Endeavour Wharf, and 15 at the Esk Wharf. Early in the 20th century Whitby was part of the great circuit of herring ports, as the shoals followed the coast down the North Sea, and it was said to be possible to walk from side to side of the harbour on the decks of herring boats. From the middle of the 18th century Whitby was a famous and successful Arctic whaling port, hunting the Greenland whale for its whalebone, and for blubber, much of which was processed further up-river. As the northern whale-fishery was 'fished out', a familiar concept, so the trade ended. The last two whalers fitted out in Whitby set sail in 1837. One was driven under the east cliff in a gale, and the other came back empty.

The Esk had other uses; it produced fish, the cockles and mussels which gathered round harbour posts, and which were used as food and as bait, the flat fish caught by small boys, which were a valuable supplement to a family's diet, and the crabs in the harbour mud. It also nurtured large scale river fisheries, at Ruswarp and at Sleights, in the days of the abbey. There are few details of their functioning, but they were valuable enough to be recorded in the dissolution documents, and to be the subject of lawsuits in the last contentious days of the abbey.

At the height of the whaling industry, there were blubber-houses processing the blubber from whales into prized whale-oil, for lamps and for lubrication, and after the 1820s for gas for street and domestic lighting. After the whaling came to a close in 1837, the Whitby Whale Oil and Gas Company became the Whitby Coal Gas Company, still on the same site.

There were mills on the river, both for grinding corn and for fulling cloth, at Ruswarp, Cock Mill and other unidentified places. One of these goes back to pre-*Domesday* times. Four mills, one a 'walk' mill, or fulling mill, are mentioned in the dissolution papers. The last surviving mill was at Ruswarp, rebuilt by the Cholmleys in 1752, with weir and mill-race, though these have not been used to drive the mill, now converted to housing, for some years. The weir provided the tide barrier, and the upper limit of the Port of Whitby.

The railway from Pickering was opened in 1836. Built by George Stephenson, it followed the river Esk from Grosmont to the estuary. At the near ox-bow in Ruswarp Fields the river was diverted, leaving the medieval ridge and furrow fields on the west side instead of the east. The later railway from Scarborough along the coast to Whitby crossed both the river, and the first railway, on an imposing viaduct where the river funnelled into Whitby. It produced a spectacular view worthy of the great painters of the industrial revolution, as railways, gasworks, river and shipping met.

The river is fed along its full length by tributaries, and there are three in the tidal reach, Cock Beck, which is below Ruswarp, Spital Beck, and Bagdale Beck. Bagdale Beck is now culverted for its last mile or so, and feeds into the Dock End, which is a refuge for smaller fishing vessels beside the larger commercial wharf. Spital Beck was the original upper limit of the port, until 1724, and Cock Beck drove one of the abbey mills. As well as tributaries, there are springs, too many of them at times, carrying Henrietta Street into the harbour in 1785, and rotting floors in the New Chapel in Baxtergate in 1783, only five years after it was built. They gave names to streets, Spring Hill, and Spring Vale, and fed Whitby's three spas, one at the foot of the east cliff, one on the site of the present Spa Theatre on the west cliff, and the still extant Victoria Spa at the back of Broomfield Terrace. These brought visitors seeking 'the waters' in the 19th century, but their influence was far more subtle than that, for they gave Whitby ample clean drinking water, they carried away detritus, and where they surfaced they flushed the gullies of the town to the fast-flowing river. The parish registers of Whitby show surprising low mortality for a town as tightly congested as Whitby was. The abundant fresh water made Whitby a relatively healthy town in historic times.

The mouth of the river is now between the west and east piers, constructions which have been altered and extended over many centuries to steer shipping safely in and out of the harbour, and to protect the town from the sea and the harbour from silting. That there was a piermaster in 1301 indicates that there was some kind of pier. This was probably the former 'Burgess Pier' now known as Tate Hill Pier. It was the first east pier, and recent archaeological investigation confirms it as medieval. Five years later the Crown granted to the abbot *quayage*, the right to levy a toll on ships for the maintenance of a quay for unloading vessels. Other such grants were made at intervals throughout the middle ages.

In the 1530s wills imply the beginnings of new works on the pier, probably of timber. A petition to Parliament at the end of the 17th century asked for an Act for a new pier to prevent the harbour from silting up. That bill was thrown out because of stiff opposition from other ports, including Scarborough and Ipswich, whose dominance of the north-east coal trade was being seriously challenged by the growing Whitby fleet. However, five years later the Act was passed, and brought with it the coveted status of 'harbour of refuge'. The piers were altered and improved over the next two hundred years. Lighthouses were built, the west in 1840 and the east in 1854, and the present extensions added in the early years of this century. The present pier extensions enable the landsman, as he walks in towards the town as dusk falls, and the lights of the town begin to show, to have some notion of the view which returning seamen obtain of the town and harbour. The fish pier, built at the turn of the 18th century, provided additional landing space, and various quays and wharves have been developed during this century.

Despite the piers, the harbour bar is still dangerous in certain conditions of wind and tide, and Reed's *Eastern Almanac* is unequivocal about the problems of trying to enter Whitby harbour;

'NOTE: No attempt should be made to enter Whitby Harbour in gales from N to NE, for then the sea breaks a long way off-shore and renders the approach dangerous.'

Whitby has had a lifeboat station on the lower harbour since 1826. There have been many heroic episodes in the station's life, including the great disaster of 1861, in which all but one of the exhausted crew of the rowing lifeboat died when it was capsized on their sixth launch within a single day to the aid of ships being driven ashore in a fearsome storm. In 1881 the survivor, Henry Freeman, became the hero, as coxswain, of a later drama, when the boat was overlanded through heavy snowdrifts to Robin Hood's Bay, some six miles away, to rescue the crew of a stranded brig, the *Visitor*.

On the banks of the River Esk, at 9 am. on every Ascension Eve, takes place a ceremony known as the Horngarth or Penny Hedge. On behalf of the tenant of a certain holding of land a simulated hedge is built on the exposed mud - Ascension being a moveable feast, the tide is always low - and a horn blast is blown. The hedge must stand for three tides. The origins of this small ceremony are lost, though there is reference to *Horngarth* as a due for certain land holdings in different parts of the Liberty. There are legends about it being a penance for the murder of a hermit, and each year it attracts a crowd. Whatever its origins, it is a remarkable survival of the services which tenants had to do in return for the land they tilled and pastured during the middle ages. Two of the few remaining manor courts which still meet in England are those of the abbey manors of Fylingdale and Whitby Lathes.

9 The Early Development of the Piers

10 The later pier development

11 The 'iron man' on the east pier

12 The harbour from Larpool

13 An eighteenth century print of an early drawbridge

14 Sutcliffe's photograph of a print of a later bridge

15 The newer of the two bridges over Spital beck.

16 A steamship on the stocks at Turnbull and Scott's shipyard at Whitehall

17 Whitby's first harbour tugs were paddle steamers

CHAPTER 4

DOWN TO THE SEA IN SHIPS

Crossing the Bar, the title of one of Tennyson's best loved poems, has for centuries been the routine experience of the men, and the watching and waiting women, of Whitby. The sight of a fishing boat heaving over into the rough waters of the open sea, or indeed, the relief, as the fishing fleet, attended by the lifeboat, reaches safety without being swept round on to Whitby Rock, the shale reef below the east cliff, is still heart-stopping, even though the crews themselves may appear quite nonchalant as they go about their business.

Faced with the alternative of a twenty-mile walk or ride across the moors to the next town, it is not surprising that the people of Whitby took to the sea. It was the quickest and cheapest way of moving goods and passengers until the railway came. Moreover, the sea was itself a source of food, bountifully available to anyone who fished. The Abbot might levy a toll on fish-landing, and demand a tithe, or tenth part, of all that was caught, but the fish would be abundant, and the only inhibitor would be the weather. That can still prevent the fishing fleet from sailing, so that Whitby may be short of fish in bad weather, and bad weather can last for days or even weeks. Now, of course, the management of declining fish stocks, and European Union quotas, have altered the sea-going pattern of the smaller, but much more technologically advanced fishing fleet.

It was not only the weather which interfered with Whitby's fishing fleet; in time of war it was relatively easy to blockade the port of Whitby, ostensibly to inhibit its merchant fleet, but in practice seriously affecting its fishing. A revealing correspondence with the Crown in 1666, beseeches the aid of the navy against a blockading French ship. The excuse is used that it is impossible to ship out alum, a crown monopoly, but when the blockade was driven away, it was the fishing fleet which took advantage of it. Blockades and other hazards during the War of American Independence raised timber prices so much that the cost of the new chapel escalated by twenty-eight per cent in a year. These same episodes, and the wars which caused them, could double the wages of the seamen who had to run the gauntlet of such blockades, economic effects on the town. An able seaman's mor from £2.00. to £4.50. in the early 18th century wars.

When Peter de Lincoln sailed overseas with the 1320s, it was very likely in his own ship, even if tha. owned. His crew would be paid the standard wages of the time, with a share in the 'freight'. They would be paid in part at the outset of the voyage, but the remainder of their contracted wages would be withheld until they returned to Whitby. They would sail under a set of rules called 'The Laws of Oléron', which were drawn up on the orders of King Richard I at the end of the 12th century, to bring the northern trades into alignment with those of the Mediterranean.

These laws are still the basis of all maritime law. If a crewman went ashore in port, he had to leave his bed on board, or forfeit part of his wages. If he died at sea, then his wages had to be paid to his next of kin. The Laws hint at the pattern of ship ownership which became standard for many centuries. Ships were held in shares, usually divisible into 4ths, 8ths, 16ths, or 32nds, until the Merchant Shipping Act of 1854 fixed the divisions as 64ths, a figure which already existed in practice, and which persists today. This shared ownership also shared the risk, from foundering, shipwreck, incompetence, piracy, mutiny and war. The principal owner was usually the one who had initiated the purchase or building of the vessel, and who, as documentation proliferated, became the managing owner, or 'ship's husband'.

The exact tonnage and design of Peter de Lincoln's ship is impossible to guess. It would probably, by the standards of later centuries, be small. The navigation would be primitive by modern standards. Much of it would be 'pilotage', achieved by taking bearings on known cliffs and buildings on the coast. Whitby's abbey was a major 'sea-mark' on this dangerous coast. 'Blue-water' sailing would be achieved by using a lodestone compass, and a primitive kind of backstaff for estimating position by the sun and stars. Much navigation tended as far as possible to stay within sight of the coast, with all its dangers of reefs and sandbanks, and open sea voyages from Whitby at this time would be largely to north-western Europe, with some Mediterranean trade. Peter himself traded in wine with Bordeaux.

There are regular references to shipping in Whitby throughout the Middle Ages, whether it was being commandeered by the Crown, as when Whitby ships were ordered to Berwick to chastise the Earl of Northumberland in 1407, or carrying coals on behalf of the abbey, ring French fleets, or tangling with pirates. Throughout the period, course, there was fishing, till in Leland's eyes in 1540, it was a *great* shing port.

The beginning of the 17th century, saw a change in Whitby's fortunes. Alum shale was discovered in the cliffs west of Whitby, and a new industry began, mining the shale and processing the alum, a vital product for the cloth trade, as a fixative for dyes. Alum has medical and other virtues, but the chemistry of production was difficult and it was some years and a great deal of investment before the industry took off. However, the transport of the raw materials and the finished product gave a huge impetus to Whitby's fortunes.

The early accounts of the alum industry show that the Scots and Dutch merchant fleets seem to have carried most of the coals required for the processing, and the 'London' urine, used for its ammonia, as well as carrying away much of the output, but gradually throughout that century, there is evidence of the growth of Whitby's shipping capacity. There is anecdotal evidence that Whitby's enterprising fishermen saw an opening and converted their fishing-boats into cargo carriers, investing in larger boats, and even diversifying into the London coal trade as opportunity arose. At the very end of the century, a Bill was laid before Parliament to enable the port to levy tolls in order to build a new pier. The Bill recorded, somewhat optimistically, it must be said, a harbour capacity for 500 ships. However, other evidence suggests that the town owned more than 100 ships of more than 200 tons burthen.

In the same century the Quaker Jonas Haggas's will and probate inventory show that his shipping interests had multiplied themselves tenfold. When Jonas's friend Francis Knaggs died in 1701, he left in realty and personalty some £935; of that some £540 was in property, including his timber yard, and of the rest £300 was invested in ship-ownership, shares in nine vessels of varying sizes. In all but one he owned either one 32nd or one 34th, but he owned half of what was described as his *fly-boat* and its stock, a total share worth £180. On the other hand, in the same year, Mary Noble, widow, died worth £34 8s 6d. Of that £15 represented a 1/32nd part of one ship and £6 was invested in a 1/64th part of a kinsman's 'pink'. That was courageous use of her widow's mite! Certainly, it would have brought an income, but, as Jonas Haggas's appraisers said in his inventory, shipping at sea was 'hazardous'.

There was little insurance for ships themselves until well into the 18th century, or for the cargoes before 1720. Thomas Barry's Lloyds' insurance book for the 1820s shows the use of underwriters to spread the risk, rather than relying on multiple ownership, with the maximum stake being £200. For the voyage of an East Indiaman, and Whitby built ships for, and sailed in, the East India trade, there might be freight worth £5,000, shared amongst twenty-five 'Names'.

The voyages of Whitby ships are surprisingly well recorded. The Seamen's Sixpence returns, for the upkeep of Greenwich Hospital for the Royal Navy, and, from 1747, for the provincial merchant seamen's hospitals, are extant. As the Sixpence was paid for every man for each month of each voyage, then these returns give good details of crew sizes, time spent at sea, and voyages made. In addition, most of the muster rolls from which these returns were made are preserved by the Seamen's Hospital in Whitby. These are often much more detailed than the enrolled returns so that from 1747 to 1818 there is a great deal of information about Whitby shipping movements and crews. Whitby's Seamen's Hospital charity for 'distressed and decayed' seamen and their dependants was established in 1675, and the elegant frontage created by Gilbert Scott conceals the original almshouses.

The early sea career of James Cook, first as a 'servant' to John Walker, the Quaker ship-owner, then as a seaman, and finally as a Mate before Cook left Whitby in 1755 to enlist in the Royal Navy, a not unusual thing for an ambitious young mariner to do, is revealed in these musters. The brilliance of Cook's fame distracts from the achievements of the other young sea apprentices of Whitby, and it is easy, therefore, to think of him as unique. Indeed he had qualities which set him far ahead of his contemporaries, but as a young man he was one of 36 apprentices serving Walker at this time, and he did not exist, or study, in a vacuum. There were in Whitby many ship-owners, all with large numbers of servants, and there were also teachers of navigation and mathematics, for such skills were essential, both for building and for sailing ships.

The best known of these teachers is Lionel Charlton, whose *History of Whitby* is such a useful early source of information. Whitby's 'products' in the 18th century were ships, and the services of the skilled navigators and seamen who sailed them. It was not only Cook who went to the Navy; ships and men were frequently hired as transports and their crews, particularly the specially-built vessels which could carry high-bulk, low-value cargoes such as coal, and the hold and deck cargoes of timber and long masts from the Baltic. Such vessels are often described in accounts of Cook's voyages as 'catts', but the term 'catt' was never used in the north-east, and is not a correct description of north-east built vessels.

The type of hull construction meant that these sturdy vessels could be used just as easily off a beach as in a deep water harbour. It was this strength which enabled *Endeavour* to survive the Great Barrier Reef on Cook's first voyage to Australia. It was that same strength which allowed the *Phoenix*, in which the Whitby historian Robert Tate Gaskin's father was a crewman, to survive being driven on to an iceberg during a furious gale. The ship was kept afloat, miraculously, and reached her home port. So damaged was she that on the very next day she began to sink at her moorings. Yet Gaskin records that during the eighty years of the whale fishery, between about 1750 and the end of the 1830s, only 13 Whitby whaling ships were lost.

The same whaling trade which was so important to the economy of Whitby in the second half of the 18th century and the first 30 years of the 19th, produced two other outstanding seamen, William Scoresby senior, and his son, William junior. Both served their time as servants in the whaling trade. William senior invented the crow's nest, that great saver of seamen's health and lives, and brought back to Whitby the record tonnage of blubber for any voyage to the Arctic. William junior's brilliant scientific mind led to his membership of the Royal Society for his work on magnetic compasses, and on the Arctic, into whose northern limits his father's ship, with William junior as Mate, had penetrated farther - only 510 miles from the Pole - than any other sailing ship had done. William Scoresby junior eventually left the sea to became an Anglican priest, becoming, in due course, Vicar of Bradford, but never losing his interest in navigation and science.

Not all seamen became mariners, that is trained able seamen and navigators, likely to become sea officers. Many spent a few years at sea, then, perhaps on marriage, took work ashore. The nature of seamen's pay meant that a seaman who was provident could have a little nest egg to invest, perhaps in a small business. Even for the officers, seafaring, because of the great physical strain of the work, was in peacetime a young man's job. There were those whose pay lasted as far as the nearest tavern, and who, having no other skill, must then sign on again for another voyage, and who might end their days broken down and pauperised, or even dying, worn out, at sea.

Men were attracted to the sea because of the opportunities afforded for work, in a society in which, at least in the 17th and 18th centuries, there was much hidden under-employment. The sea offered a bed, regular food, work, and a lump sum in payment. Seamen had the legal right to carry a little personal cargo on board, and there was also the opportunity to smuggle small amounts of contraband goods. Indeed, attempts in the early 19th century to tighten the rules about small-scale smuggling brought enraged protests from respectable Societies of Shipowners in the north east as this small perquisite was threatened.

Not all smuggling was *into* the port. About 1702 the then Rector of Sneaton, near Whitby, later described in the Consistory Court as 'a notorious drunkard and brawler', endeavoured to bribe two coblemen to take his pregnant housekeeper and mistress to the master of a Whitby ship standing off-shore, so that she might be abandoned in London. The men, to their credit, refused, and the mistress found friends who helped to bring the Rector before the Consistory Court, and to obtain provision for herself and the child.

For the ambitious young seaman there was also, as an inducement, the possibility of social advancement. In 1800 William Douglas sailed, as a fifteen-year-old servant, on the *George* to Riga to load timber. He became, like so many seamen, a prisoner of the unstable Tsar Paul I. William was the eldest son of an illiterate seaman, but his mother was literate, and her son was indentured as a servant, and, having survived his imprisonment in Russia, he had become a master mariner by the time he himself married at the age of 26. As a master he had become middle-class, eligible for all the honours of that status.

He might invest his pay in shipping, and become an owner; he might happen upon a prize in time of war, having taken out 'Letters of Marque', as Whitby masters did, and with guns aboard be permitted to do a little privateering, although few Whitby vessels were successful at it. He might be invited to sit upon the multifarious committees of Whitby's mercantile life; the Marine Society; the Seamen's Hospital; the Marine Insurance Society. He might become a freemason, or he might aspire to civic office. He might, on the other hand, be lost at sea. Research shows that about one third of all masters died at sea when their ships were lost. Although many Whitby-built ships remained sea-worthy for up to a century, it is estimated that in the days of sail about four per cent of British shipping was lost each year. The principal risks were of foundering in a storm, or of being wrecked, by driving ashore or onto rocks, usually in a gale, but at times by incompetence. Fire was a great hazard in wooden ships, well-tarred, and carrying large amounts of spare canvas, timber and cordage. Sometimes, in the heavy fogs of the east coast, small ships were run down by larger, and the parish registers record a higher number of dead seamen washed ashore in summer, during the 'sea-fret' season, than in winter. Most of the disbursements of the charitable societies for officers and men in Whitby went to widows. There were times when Whitby profited from wrecks, by salvage, and sometimes illicitly, as in 1352, when the men of Whitby, including the Abbot, were accused of removing a cargo of white herrings from a ship of Boston broken up on the shore.

Not all distress was caused by death. There was a high risk of physical injury and maiming in the merchant fleet. Men fell from slippery yards in gales, ice and rain; they were backlashed by parting ropes and cables, and above all they suffered from abdominal hernia. As ship technology improved, the manning levels of merchant ships dropped so that the tonnage per man in the crew of the *George* in 1800 was 28 tons, and much of the ship's work was by manpower, as they struggled to harness the power of wind and water.

James Cook deliberately joined the navy in 1755, and so did others from the merchant service. The navy was less dependent on economic factors for its crew levels, and N.A.M. Rodgers' book *The Wooden World* demonstrates many of the advantages to be gained by an ambitious young seaman. But others joined reluctantly, possibly because wages in the merchant fleet were much higher than in the navy. The pressgang took an active interest in Whitby from the 17th century onwards, generally as a recruiting service, when its principal opponents were probably owners and seamen's wives, but in times of extreme pressure, as in the Napoleonic Wars, as a hunting and conscripting body. Whitby's trained seamen were a great prize, far preferable to any landsman.

Indeed outside fiction it was a desperate Impress Lieutenant who took landsmen. Whitby's long confrontation with the pressgangs reached its climax in 1793, with a riot, destruction of the pressgang rendezvous, and in due course, a hanging at York, and a transportation to Botany Bay. In earlier times it had its funny side when an impress agent, Thomas Shipton, in Whitby in 1666 wrote frantic letters to the Navy Board for a ship to come and take all the men he had carefully gathered in Hull and Scarborough before they ran away.

The sea provided Whitby with most of its economic resource from the 16th century, and probably before, but there was a darker side. The North Sea had more than its fair share of pirates, some of them, of course, from Whitby. There are recorded incidents of raids from the sea, by Norsemen who burned abbey and town in the 12th century, by Scots who raided the abbey, and particularly the abbey's cattle, deer and sheep, and by individual pirates who captured ships and cast away their crews. In 1311 two Dunkirk pirate ships attacked a ship called *Blith*, threw the crew overboard and took away their prize. In an even more brazen raid within the harbour, in 1327, 38 people on board a ship were murdered and the ship seized. In the same year Peter de Lincoln lost a cargo of Bordeaux wine with his ship the *St Mary Bote*. Once the abbot was accused of piracy, when a 'taken' Danish ship was brought into the harbour in the 16th century, and the abbot joined in the general disposal of its contents. His excuse was that there had been great want in the community that year past.

In 1626, during the war with Spain, Mrs. Elizabeth Cholmley shipped the family's household valuables from London for Whitby, only to have them taken by a 'Dunkirker' - the ports of Dunkirk and Ostend were notorious for pirates. The Cholmleys were doubly unlucky, for the possessions which were being shipped back to England in 1647 from their exile in France were lost to an Ostend pirate.

Not all of those on board ships were seamen; ships carried carpenters, to maintain the vessel, and particularly its water casks. A whaler, which carried extra barrels for packing the blubber, might also have a cooper as a crewman. Ship's carpenters might lead a double life, working sometimes on ships and at other times in the shipyards, where the same skills were needed. But the craftsmen who built the ships, made the masts and spars, and fashioned the blocks also did other woodwork in the town, and many of Whitby's land-bound buildings carry their trademarks. The roof of St Mary's Church is the roof of a ship's cabin, light, watertight and affording a good view, if one could reach it. The galleries, as in St Ninian's Church, are supported by pillars of fine pine, exactly the kind of wood that was made into masts, and, after 200 years, without a vestige of a twist. The pillars in the parish church have been lovingly marbled by some long-gone painter and decorator to hide their workaday origins, but in fact they stand as a memorial to several centuries of fine ship technology.

Less obvious in the same church are the graffiti on seats occupied by generations of apprentices and servants as they whiled away sermon time by carving fine pictures of ships inside the box pews, which of course afforded excellent cover for such activities. Seafaring penetrated every part of life in Whitby.

Ashore the fleet was served by a range of dedicated facilities. As well as the ship-repair yards, sail-cloth manufacturers and other major enterprises, there were smaller firms which dealt in chandlery and marine stores in general. Whitby vessels in the coastal trade, and fishing vessels, - diminished to nine in the 18th century, but much more numerous in the peak of the herring industry - and visiting merchant ships all needed supplies, and these were readily available. Browne Bushell, victualling his ship *John* in 1632 had bought an ox, had it killed, then butchered and salted down, selling the hide to offset costs, but the growing fleet required a less do-it-yourself system, and a proper infrastructure grew up, expanding and contracting as need arose.

Among the facilities necessary in any port were inns and ale-houses, to provide recreation for crews, and to offer accommodation to those awaiting a berth. They were very variable in quality and facilities, led by the early 19th century Angel Hotel, the highest-rated building in the town, far more valuable that any of the ship-owners' houses at the time. That was much more of a social centre for the whole town, having facilities for meetings. In the Angel was held the meeting which in 1831 planned the railway between Whitby and Pickering, and brought great changes to the town. It is perhaps typical of Whitby's necessarily matriarchal society that this important hub was presided over and owned by Miss Esther Yeoman.

Coaching inns were an important part of urban life, with their entrances just big enough to accommodate the carefully manoeuvred horses and the lumbering coach behind. The White Horse and Griffin in Church Street was such an inn, serving the passengers who came on the regular coaches which connected Whitby overland to the wider world, before the railway came. It still has its coach yard and outbuildings behind, and is still a hotel.

Smaller public houses came and went. There are still many in the old town. Some grew notorious for their association with the hated pressgang who would set up the 'rendezvous' within an ale-house to entrap the unwary seaman. Others, like the present-day 'Smuggler' in Baxtergate, metamorphosed into genteel teashops. Much of their function was taken over by the new hotels and boarding-houses built on the west cliff to accommodate the middle-class visitors brought by the new railway. Some like the Middle Earth Tavern in Church Street have changed their names to serve a much more modern clientele. One or two have became the focus of music, especially during Whitby's well-known folk week in August. All are very busy during the summer season, especially during Whitby's Regatta, bringing them round once again to their function to serve the port.

18 The great terror of the days of sail was to be close to the land in an 'on-shore' gale

19 Even steamers could come to grief on a lee-shore if their engines failed

20 Henry Freeman

21 Saltwick Bay and Black Nab

22 Women's work: women and girls gathering flithers or limpets

23 The herring fleet setting out under sail

24 The 166 ton brig *Opal* at the New Quay

25 The two parallel sheds at the Spital Bridge ropewalk

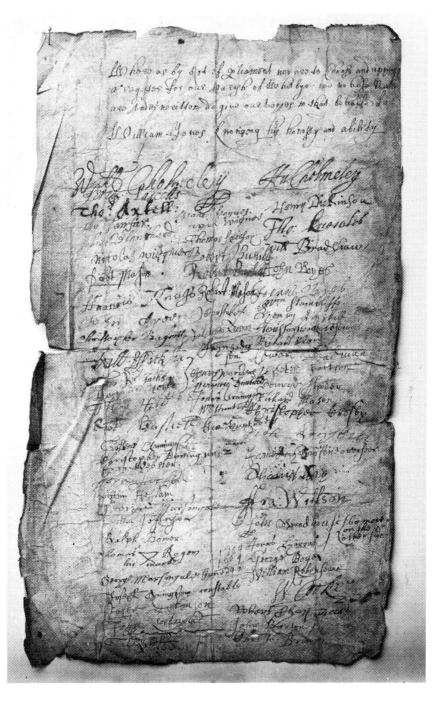

26 Sutcliffe photographed this parchment inserted into the parish register during the Commonwealth period, 1653-1660.

CHAPTER 5

WARS AND RUMOURS OF WARS

Whitby, or *Streoneshalh*, was conceived and born of war. St Hilda herself was born an exile in the kingdom of Elmet, whose rulers had killed her father, and was probably named Hilda to signify her need to struggle. Her great-uncle, King Edwin, who became the first Christian king of Northumbria, spent much of his life struggling to maintain his kingdom, and after his death in battle his body was brought to Whitby for burial, a few miles from the resting place of the loyal thane, Lilla, who gave his life to save Edwin from an earlier assassin, and whose name is commemorated in Lilla Cross, one of the remarkable crosses found on the Moors, and an ancient boundary marker for the Liberty of the abbey.

Hilda's kinsman, King Oswy, promised God before his battle with the heathen King Penda of Mercia, that if he, Oswy, was successful against Penda, he would give his infant daughter to God, and would found ten monasteries in gratitude for God's help. In thanksgiving after Penda's death, and the end of a twenty year struggle, Oswy gave his daughter Ælfleda into the care of Hilda, then Abbess at Hartlepool, and sent them both to *Streoneshalh*.

Long after her death, Hilda's abbey, dedicated to St Peter, declined as power shifted south from the Northumbrian kingdom and England was unified. Yet enough remained above the ground, so the abbey Chronicle said, for a Norman knight, Reinfrid, probably serving on the savage campaign which laid waste the north of England after the Conquest, to be touched by it, and to become a monk and refound the monastery on land given by another soldier, William de Percy, who himself died in Palestine on the First Crusade, between 1095 and 1099. The early days of the Norman abbey were beset by war, as the coast was attacked by Norwegian invaders, and the newly formed monastery retreated to Hackness. There were other raids from the sea, though the exact dates are not always clear.

Throughout the middle ages Whitby was, as are all coastal ports, a frontier town. Though well south of the present border, and buffered by the palatinate of the Prince-Bishop of Durham, it was nevertheless vulnerable at times even by land, since the Scots showed a disinclination to stay behind their border. The Battle of the Standard, fought in 1138 near Northallerton, was a long way south of Whitby. The sea, however, really was a frontier, against many enemies, both of the state and of the abbey and town.

Not all Scots, of course, came in war, and the 1301 taxation of Whitby includes a taxpayer from Mussleburgh; moreover, one of the early benefactors of the abbey, endowing the cell at Middlesbrough, was Peter de Brus, founder of Guisborough Priory, whose descendant, Robert the Bruce, became King of Scots in 1306. One of Bruce's predecessors, David I of Scots, had confirmed grants of land near Kelso in Scotland to Whitby abbey.

There were, however, fairly frequent episodes of conflict between England and Scotland, including the Wars of Scottish Independence, and Whitby became involved in those. The town had to provide ships to fight the Scots, as did thirty or forty other English ports. Sometimes the town, in common with other ports, was banned from trading with certain foreign powers, as alliances fluctuated. Peter de Lincoln's safe-conducts in the 1320s were licences to conduct his affairs overseas in time of conflict. The abbot, who held a considerable benefice at Crosseby in Cumberland, had to send supplies to Carlisle and other northern strongholds to fight against the Scots. The taxations at the turn of the 14th century were to finance Scots wars, between King Edward I and Robert the Bruce. Was the Abbot, handsomely endowed by de Brus of Danby and Skelton, suspected of sympathy with de Brus of Annandale?

Border wars brought the court north, and increased the abbey's dealings with the Crown. The surviving transactions were much more numerous during the Scottish wars. The Scots' alliance with France also brought conflict, and French ships were captured during the wars with France, notably when the French fleet was taken in 1451

During the 15th century, when a hundred years of successive minorities among the Stuart Kings of Scots brought lawlessness to the Borders, Scottish "visitations" became much more troublesome and less structured. But not only Scots raided Whitby, and one visit by a band of Yorkshiremen from as far as Nidderdale, and as near as Sandsend, in 1404, relieved the abbot of all his cattle, his sheep and the deer from his park in Fyling Dale. The catchment wall of the park still stands, a monument to the medieval art of emparking and holding wild deer. The abbot complained bitterly to the king.

Evidence of Scottish raids is found in the Papal archives, as the abbot pleaded for remission of dues because of the terrible raids of the Scots. There is, sadly, no evidence to say how bad these were, or whether they were merely an excuse to avoid paying taxes to the Papal State. Sometimes there was retribution, as in 1439, when a Scotsman, lying, apparently in the abbey prison, in Whitby, wrote pleadingly to the Prior of St Andrews, offering the Prior his house in that town in return for money to be remitted to Whitby to save his life.

Not all these warlike episodes related to foreign wars. The rebellion against King John, which led to his signing of *Magna Carta*, involved some of the abbot's feudal tenants, and Abbot Roger de Scarborough was eventually a witness to the reissued *Magna Carta* when it was confirmed by Henry III. In 1403 the Earl of Northumberland, father of Shakespeare's 'Hotspur', became involved in rebellion against King Henry IV, and it was the port of Whitby which was ordered to send ships to Berwick to 'chastise' him. But the Earl was High Steward of Whitby Abbey, in receipt of feudal dues from the abbot. It was the town and not the abbey which provided the ships, but the irony cannot have escaped the protagonists.

There were passive aspects of war which also affected the abbey. In 1383, King Richard II required a survey to be made of Mulgrave Castle, both of the estate, and all its water, bridges, weirs and other appurtenances, and of the castle and its capacity as a fortification. He asked the abbot to do this service. It seems quite sensible that the abbot, who was a great landowner, should be expected to survey the estates, but it is interesting that he was also expected to be competent to make judgements on the castle and fortifications. It is often said that the prelates of the medieval church had become very worldly, and yet at times that worldliness was thrust upon them. The Abbot of Whitby could be summoned to sit in the King's councils, or to undertake responsible tasks on behalf of the Crown, and there could be no refusal.

The Pilgrimage of Grace, raised by Robert Aske and others against the King Henry VIII's attack on the monasteries in 1536, came near to causing disaster at the abbey. The abbot, John Hexham, managed to steer a very difficult course. Despite being accused of lending aid to the rebellion, (under duress, he maintained), he kept his head, but retired early, leaving the space for the King's nominee, Henry Divall, the last abbot.

The post-reformation period brought new hazards to the town. The Spanish Armada passed by without leaving wreckage or prizes, but the paranoia was doubtless there, particularly as there was a high proportion of recusant Roman Catholics in the area, including the lord of the manor, Henry Cholmley, whose wife had been born a Catholic. In the days of the Elizabethan persecutions, Catholic seminary priests entered England through Whitby, despite the risks, knowing that there was safe refuge with the Cholmleys.

The 17th century brought peace from the Scots, when the Crowns of England and Scotland were united in 1603, but at the same time brought new alliances, and new conflicts. King James VI and I tried to avoid wars, but his son King Charles I became embroiled in Europe, and his reign led to the civil wars which had serious effects on Whitby. When Scarborough Castle, under the governorship of Sir Hugh Cholmley, fell to parliament in 1645, Cholmley went into exile, though his wife and children were permitted to remain in Whitby. The port of Whitby, which supported parliament, was also captured by Sir Thomas Fairfax, thus finally denying any port facilities in the north-east to the king. The Navigation Ordinances and Acts passed during and after the Commonwealth period affected shipping, by bringing war with the Dutch, whose predominance in overseas trade was threatened by the Acts. One result was a blockade of Whitby by Dutch vessels, in 1666, as well as visits from the pressgang. There were prizes, too, as always in a largely naval war, though this could have a very adverse effect on ship-building, as an inordinate number of 'prizes', combined with the ending of war, and consequent release of naval transports, and even warships, into the mercantile economy, could cause serious slumps in the ship-building ports.

In the 18th and early 19th centuries Britain was frequently at war, with consequent effects on Whitby. The 18th century began with the War of the Spanish Succession, and wars were frequent until 1815. It was a period which brought prosperity and not a little fame, to the port of Whitby. Whitby began the 18th century with the much-needed Act of Parliament which enabled the building of the piers which in turn led to the expansion of Whitby's activities, and thus enabled the use of Whitby ships as transports by the navy; this same Act gave opportunity for John Walker's prosperity, and was perhaps the accidental cause of his taking a young apprentice called James Cook; Cook joined the Navy during the Seven Years' War, and was the hydrographer who surveyed the St Lawrence River, and enabled Wolfe to take Quebec. That in turn led to Cook's appointment to sail to the south seas to study the Transit of Venus, and to his charting of the coasts of Australia and New Zealand, and his eventual death in 1779 on his third voyage.

Another war, the War of American Independence, led to the perceived need for a new penal colony to replace those in America, and Cook's work enabled the settlement of Botany Bay, and the founding of Australia, but Whitby-built ships were involved in that as well, as two, the *Fishburn* and the *Golden Grove*, sailed as transports with that fleet, and gave us, through the logs of their circumnavigation, some further insight into the experiences of the kind of ship built in Whitby yards when faced by the worst excesses of the southern seas.

Not all Whitby's heroes were sailors, and in St Mary's parish church there is a memorial tablet to a man whose military career spanned much of the century, till his death, in his bed, in 1772 at the age of 87. General Peregrine Lascelles was born in Staithside in Whitby, and became a professional soldier, serving four monarchs in that capacity. His tablet lists his campaigns and battles, including the 'dreadful rout' of Prestonpans, when the government troops fled the field in the face of Prince Charles Edward Stuart's highlanders. Lascelles had tried to hold ground, but was deserted by his men, and narrowly escaped. He seems to have been much loved for qualities which are carefully listed, and the long epitaph ends, 'in short, an Honest Man'.

The deaths of individual Whitby men in war are sometimes revealed in their wills, and there is a recurrent thread of this in the probate documents of the ecclesiastical Provinces of Canterbury and York. Sometimes these men died as a result of enemy action while on a merchant ship, but at times they died while in the navy, as in 1740 when at least three Whitby men died on board HMS *Superb* in the Mediterranean, and their inventories record small possessions and pay due. During the wars of the 18th and 19th century the French captured Whitby ships, after long chases up the North Sea, and occasionally, of course, captured French ships were brought into Whitby. There were French prisoners in Whitby during the Napoleonic Wars, and French prizes were re-registered as Whitby ships. The newspapers of the time, particularly the *Hull Packet* and the *Hull Advertiser,* record several such events.

Whitby ships were hired as *transports* by the navy, to carry stores or soldiers to overseas theatres of action, and sometimes these ships foundered or were sunk by enemy action. Even under convoy, which always proceeded at the speed of the slowest vessel, a straggler could lag behind and be picked off. The problems of keeping ships together under sail are well illustrated by the signals of the flagship of the First Fleet to the *Golden Grove*, which had a distinct tendency to labour and lag behind, while her sister ship the *Fishburn*, if we are to believe her master, was frequently told to shorten sail and slow down.

Perhaps the most dramatic wartime adventure which befell Whitby seamen took place on land, in the winter of 1800-1801, when Tsar Paul I, for various ill-conceived reasons, placed an embargo on the British ships which were in Russian ports. These ships were taken captive, and their crews sent ashore. The ships were in Russian ports to buy and load vital raw materials for ship-building for the war against Napoleon. Paul had been a subscriber to the 'Second Coalition' against Napoleon, but his allegiance began to waver.

Embargoes were fairly routine actions in wartime among enemies, and crews would normally expect to be taken off the ships, and imprisoned locally until either freed or exchanged. Tsar Paul, however, embargoed allied ships, and then imposed an appalling fate upon the seamen. They were divided into groups and forced to march to 102 different towns in the interior of Russia, during a long Russian winter for which they were neither clothed nor victualled. Over two hundred British ships were caught, and it has been possible to identify most of them from contemporary newspapers, though the official list has been lost. As Whitby provided about a fifth of the shipping which traded with the Baltic, it is reasonable to assume that over forty Whitby ships were captured, with about five or six hundred seamen. We know the names of many of those ships, from muster rolls, and from the records of the Russia Company. There is a detailed log, probably the only one to survive the episode, written by a young seaman called Thomas Etty as the official journal of the *George*.

Eventually, following both the assassination of Paul, and the Battle of Copenhagen, most of the seamen returned home, in their own ships, but many had died, and they had been away for well over a year. The whole incident had caused serious economic problems in Whitby, and on the rest of the north-east and Scottish coast.

Whitby town suffered during war, with guns placed on its battery at the harbour entrance, and with militiamen and fencibles quartered in the town; at times there were little local incidents, when cannon blew up, but perhaps the most drastic effects on the townscape came in the two world wars of this century. On December 16th, 1914, a German flotilla stood inshore and bombarded the abbey and the town, causing loss of life, and destruction, not only of part of the abbey ruin, but of part of the town as well. It was an experience shared by Scarborough and Hartlepool, and caused serious fears of invasion, so that many refugees fled inland. A group of girls sent home from the County School had a narrow escape on the school playing field when a warning shout from a watcher prevented them from being killed by shrapnel. The school still has the offending piece of shrapnel. It also had until recently an avenue of poplar trees, one for each old pupil killed in that war.

In the same year the hospital ship HMHS *Rohilla* was driven aground by Saltwick Nab with much loss of life, and great heroism by lifeboatmen and rescuers. The war memorials in St Mary's church reveal the sacrifice of many lives, not all at sea, and some of them women, in both world wars and in the earlier South African wars. The 1939-45 war also brought bombardment, but this time from the air, with a bombing raid which left dead and injured in Flowergate. That war also led to the blowing up of the bridges between the piers and their extensions, presumably to deter raids from the sea. It is said that the anti-aircraft batteries on the cliffs drove the seagulls from their cliff top nests to the chimneys of the town where they still nest, though not always welcome as neighbours. Even in the cold war Whitby played a small role, when the Polish fishing trawler *Puszcyk* was brought into the port in 1954 by its mutinous crew, who promptly asked for political asylum.

The visible signs remain, whether in the damaged west end of the medieval abbey ruins, the new buildings on the bomb site in Flowergate, or the cannon placed on the Battery Parade. Over the centuries the enemy has varied widely, and changed with national political alliances, and for most of the inhabitants war would be simply a matter of new discomforts and sorrows to endure, but it has been part of the pattern of life in Whitby since the first abbey grew out of a promise before the Battle of the River *Winwæd* in 656.

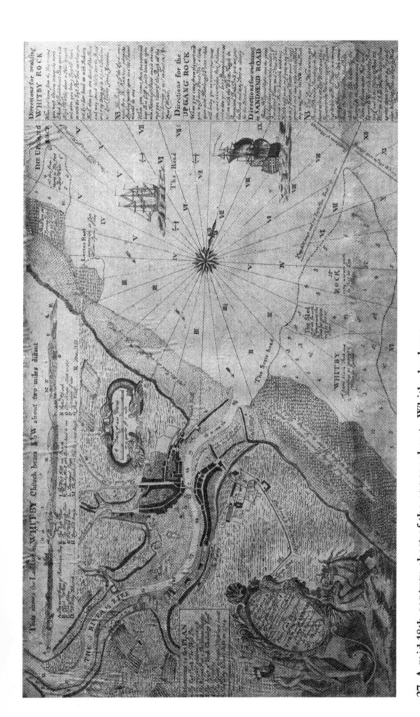

27 A mid 18th century chart of the approaches to Whitby harbour.

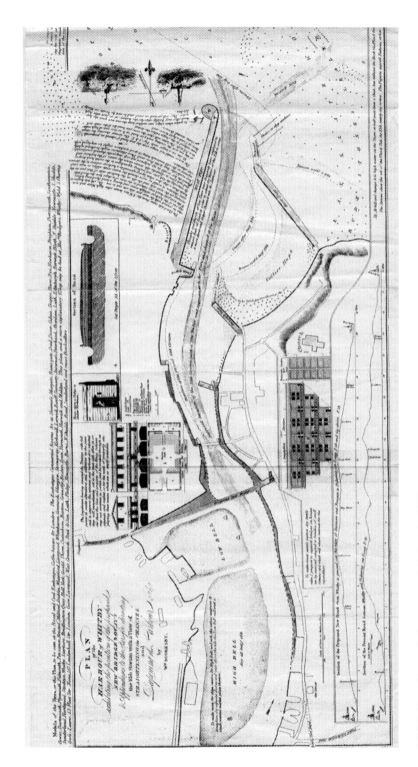

28 William Scoresby's map, published in 1818

29   The rooflines of St Mary's taken from the Abbey plain

CHAPTER 6

GOOD, BAD AND DESPERATE;
THE HANDLING OF MONEY

Probate inventories from the 17th and 18th centuries in Whitby show a very sophisticated skill in the handling of investments. The inventories listed and valued a deceased's possessions, and at the end of the inventory reference was made to debts owed to him or her, and these were often classified; as book debts, for sales or services recently rendered; as bonds, mortgages and notes of hand, for money lent at interest with proper documentation; and as sundry debts, some of them good, or likely to be repaid, or bad, which were going to be difficult to recover, or, alas, desperate, or beyond hope. Sometimes it becomes apparent that the deceased had died at a most inconvenient time, when that which he owed was temporarily greater than that which was owed to him, as with Arthur Dickinson in 1724, for the network of venture capital which kept Whitby quite literally afloat was very complex.

Sometimes early and unexpected demise might lead to the founding of fortunes. When a small boy, Jonas Haggas, aged seven, orphaned probably by plague in 1636, inherited, a year later, from his grandfather John Haggas a house and part of a small ship, he made of that a career at sea, and a fortune in land, shipping and money invested in enterprise in the town. In turn, Jonas Haggas, dying childless and widowed, left £100 to 'Deborah Vaughan as a token of my love'. That substantial windfall may well, passed on in due time, have led to the gentrification of the Vaughan family in the 18th century. At the same time £5, the equivalent of a single share in one small ship, just such a share as Jonas himself had gained as a child, left to John Walker, apprentice to Daniel Yeoman, may have contributed to the fortunes of the Quaker shipowning Walkers, whose most famous apprentice was James Cook. Haggas was himself an early member of the Society of Friends, at times refusing to pay church rates, on grounds of conscience.

There was no institutionalised finance in Whitby until the late 18th century, when several banks were established by merchants who had done some banking alongside their other business. The first is generally thought to have been that of Simpson and Chapman, who set up a bank at Greengates in Grape Lane in 1785. The beautiful town house in which they did their business still has the twin safes of that early enterprise, and on the crown glass of its famous sixty-paned 'bottle' window are scratched the signatures of early members of the banking family.

Whitby banks prospered, despite the slumps and swings in the shipping, whaling and alum industries, and their bank notes were respected, though there were traumas, as when Saunders' Bank had to suspend dealings temporarily in 1793, a difficult year, and when Campion's Bank failed in 1840. Campion's Bank itself was unusual in that it had been founded by a woman, Mrs. Margaret Campion, and her sons, in 1787. Mrs Margaret Campion must have been a redoubtable lady, for in 1795 she purchased her freedom of the Russia Company, without which she could not undertake trade with Russia, after Catherine the Great annexed the Baltic states from which Whitby shipped much of its timber. Mrs Margaret was not Whitby's only female entrepreneur. Mary Richardson was a founding partner in a bank, and Mrs Alice Reynolds was one of the original shareholders of Whitby's very entrepreneurial Chapel in Baxtergate in 1778. She and several other widows took over the running of their late husbands' ships. Women in a community from which the men were often absent for very long periods indeed, and who took a high risk of early widowhood when they married into seafaring, were accustomed to doing business, handling money and making decisions. The early censuses in Whitby and other ports designated mariners' and seamen's wives whose husbands were at sea as 'heads of household', according them a status which mirrored their necessary competence. The letters of the Watt family, held in the family archive in Orkney, include about 100 letters from James Watt, apprenticed to Jonas Brown, shipowner of Whitby, and his Whitby-born wife Elizabeth to James's family in Orkney, and give a vivid picture of the domestic and economic life of a middle-class seafaring family in 18th century Whitby.

Today it is from banks and other financial institutions that the capital for business, construction and other investments comes, yet Whitby's banking did not become institutionalised until well into the period of its greatest prosperity. Most of the enterprises in which Whitby was commercially involved from the 17th century were heavily capitalised, unlike the much more `domestic' industries of other parts of the country. While a domestically working 17th century craftsman might have 'plant' worth £5, an inventory of an alum manufactory in 1650 gave a value of over £1500, and even Francis Knaggs's 'raffins', or timber, yard, was valued at £160 in 1701.

Shipping itself was highly capitalised, as well as 'hazardous', and the cost of building and equipping ships, and of the cargoes which they carried, required a large amount of private venture capital, so that it becomes clear early in the commercial history of Whitby that the handling and disposition of venture capital was very sophisticated. Although there is little written evidence for the middle ages, the presence of a goldsmith in 1301 may indicate that there was investment, for medieval goldsmiths often acted as bankers to the town. Peter de Lincoln's voyages might involve investment from fellow citizens, and even from the abbey, which was itself engaged in the export trade in wool and herrings, so that there were several centuries of profit and loss from which to learn before the town began its rise from the middle of the 17th century. Most of the evidence for the system comes from the probate inventories, and most of those for the 18th century have been published, and show a complex use of venture capital.

Shipowners rarely owned their vessels outright, and this sharing of risk was well established by the beginning of the 17th century. Sometimes the 'managing' owner, or 'ship's husband', held only a single share in his ship, though he might acquire others if the ship proved well-found. Sometimes he would act as master of his own ship, as did Christopher Pearson of the brig *Thaïs*, so that when she was embargoed by the Russians in 1800, and he and his crew were force-marched into Russia for the winter, his loss was not only of liberty, but of income both for himself and for the ship. Small wonder that the muster roll for the voyage expressed such relief when they all finally came back on board.

The inventories give us a better view of ship owning than is to be found in other shipping documents, which often list only the managing owner, for they indicate the determination of even humble people, such as Mary Noble, to become involved in Whitby's affairs. £5 bought a small stake in great enterprise, especially in the smaller vessels such as sloops and schooners. After registration of shipping began in 1786, a clearer picture appears of the ownership at that time, with fewer owners per vessel, since insurance could carry most of the risk. Gone were the long lists of shareholders from the early 18th century.

Greater investment and sophistication shared the risk in freight, and Thomas Barry's Lloyds insurance ledgers from the 1820s show the amount of risk carried by individual underwriters to be around £200. If a cargo was worth only £400, then there would be two underwriters, but an

East Indiaman going to the Asian sub-continent round the Cape with £5,000 worth of freight had 25 underwriters. The same names appear frequently, so that it is clear that a great deal of capital had been staked by individuals, but never more than £200 in any single voyage.

Such capital had to be obtained before it could be invested, and money was often tied up in real estate, so that money was borrowed to finance these enterprises, and it is this lending and borrowing, without the use of banks, that is so complex. Much was raised by mortgages, using houses as security for loans for other ventures. Jonathan Porritt's inventory of 1764 shows the extent of his investments; he held mortgages, bonds and notes of hand, all secured loans, for £4,000, and all loaned to other business men in the town. Other inventories show the same pattern, and where the loans were individually specified, it is obvious that much of the venture capital which supported Whitby's prosperity came from within the town.

Jonathan had been a master mariner, and his money would have come from wages, from 'freight' on his own account, and from judicious trading and investment in ships and men. The loans matured, and earned interest, probably between two and five percent. Property increased in value as Whitby prospered, and Jonathan owned a good deal of property, some of which also earned rent. Ships earned money, and Jonathan Porritt had shares in ships, although fewer than one would have expected for a thriving former master mariner. Perhaps he preferred his risk to be taken at arm's length, investing money in legally protected mortgages rather than in vessels 'at sea, and hazardous'. He was a public figure, being one of the churchwardens whose names are recorded on the remains of the bell-frame in which the first peal was rung on Whitby's bells, re-hung in 1752. The re-casting and re-hanging are themselves evidence of the town's self-esteem.

The minute books of the Russia Company, the company of merchant venturers in the City of London which controlled all trade with Russia, show the extent of Whitby's involvement in the trade in Baltic timber, for there is a long list of Whitby merchants who bought the freedom of the company, and Whitby regularly sent her dues through the Collector of Customs who acted as agent for the company. Most of her trade with Russia was as a carrier of goods to the Thames, but there were steady imports into Whitby.

Ships' account books, of which Whitby Museum has a good collection, show the amount of capital that was tied up in any ship. The stores of victuals and stock for voyages, sometimes of great duration, across the principal oceans, had to be bought, and all ships carried spare parts; masts, spars, blocks, suits of sails, timber for mending the hull, ropes, metalwork, canvas for repairs, oakum for caulking; fuel for the galley fire or for melting tar and pitch; slops or clothes for the crew, barrels for oil and chaldrons for measuring coal were on board. There was fresh water, often as part of the ballast, and there were navigational instruments and charts. And without passengers or cargo, all that equipment represented dead money, all to be found before the ship earned a penny. Often ships sailed under ballast, of slate, water or gravel or some other weighty substance stowed in the hold to maintain stability, and earned nothing until they reached the Baltic, where it was the responsibility of the master, through agents, or through his own skill at networking, to find a cargo and negotiate terms. Every master had to be a shrewd negotiator, and pay his own way, either with cash or bills of exchange. If he failed, then there was no profit from the trip.

A ship might spend four months whaling in the Arctic, and come home empty, or 'clean', so that the entire investment in stores gained nothing. A glimpse of how merchant shipping dealt with the problem of providing the master with the cash to purchase stores has recently been solved by detailed research in Whitby's archives. Until insurance became commonplace and ended the need for multiple shareholders, each share holder had to provide a proportion of a cash sum called 'the stock', which could be used throughout the year to pay for victualling, small repairs and chandlery. No-one received any profit at the end of the year until the stock had been made up to its appointed total ready for the next year's trading. It was part of the fixed capital of the vessel.

Not all of Whitby's investment was in shipping, ship-building and allied occupations. The railway came to Whitby, designed by George Stephenson, and brought across the Moors from Pickering. £80,000 was raised for that from individual investors. There was investment in mining, alum mines, coal mines on the Moors, and in the iron mining and smelting industry which developed and grew during the late 18th and 19th centuries. When jet became more fashionable for jewellery after the death of the Prince Consort in 1861, Whitby, as the principal source of the mineral, developed a flourishing industry, but it was never as heavily capitalised as the older industries, being mainly carried out in small workshops, though there were some wealthy merchants. Alas, an industry built upon a fashion rather than a need brought much distress in the wake of its inevitable decline, even among the families with the largest stake in the industry. Changes in fashion also contributed to the decline of whaling, after whalebone became less 'necessary' for clothing, and the Arctic whaling industry died in the 1830s after both the loss of the government bounty on whales, and the development of other means of lighting.

In the 19th century, when railways, steam ships and iron-mining were an important part of Whitby's commercial life, and institutional banking had become well established, many Whitby people still did private business, and capital was raised publicly for local works, such as the museum, and for individual needs. In 1800 Whitby Union Mill Society was established, to grind corn at a reasonable price, and with charitable backing. By 1815 it had some 900 subscribers, and was profitable, but an element of doubt as to its dealings was creeping in. Revd. George Young, minister of the Presbyterian Church and a historian of note, expressed the concern of his circle as to whether the original intention was being followed.

Public subscription was a fashionable way to raise funds for good works, and the charity boards of the parish church give testimony to the generosity and far-sightedness of many of the wealthier citizens. Expertise in the handling of money led to the establishment of several schools for the poor and needy well before compulsory education.

There was additional investment in property in the 19th century as the town expanded on the west cliff to take in the visitors for whom Whitby had become a fashionable resort, as the railway gradually linked up with national networks. Some of these investments came from speculators such as George Hudson, the 'Railway King', of York, but many were from within the town, and some houses were built by individuals with the specific intention of letting to wealthy visitors. The letting of rooms and holiday flats is still part of Whitby's investment practice. It possibly replaced for the small investor the single share in a small ship, when these became fewer with the decline of sail and the decline of the port. Although fishing continued to be important, its financing was quite different from that of merchant shipping, and tended to be kept within the fishing community. The great steam ships which were built at Turnbull's Yard until the beginning of the 20th century were, even at 1/64th shares, quite beyond the reach of the Mary Nobles of 19th century Whitby, but taking summer visitors into her house would have been a welcome addition to the family income.

The day-to-day handling of money is well-illustrated by the building of the New Chapel, a business-like establishment built in 1778. Mr. John Holt acted as banker, holding the money raised from shares sold to 30 shareholders, receiving the accounts of the various tradesmen and creditors and disbursing the payment in the form of handwritten. 'cheques' which could then be presented for cash. Each paper is carefully preserved as a record of the transaction, together with the relevant account. Although Richardson and Holt's Bank was not established officially for some years after this, John Holt, who was himself a shareholder in the chapel, as well as a shipowner and ship-builder, was already effectively banking.

For many Whitby people investments were a principal source of income in old age, and the Census of 1851 reveals many people who are described as 'Annuitants', usually in the 'better' parts of town, such as St Hilda's Terrace, but also in other less fashionable places. They are often widows, made comfortable by their own, or their husbands' prudent use of venture capital. For many, of course, the investments were a declining resource, as shipping slumped, mines were worked out and fashions and technology changed, and genteel poverty would be the lot of those who lived too long.

The Will of John Haggas

In the Name of God Amen The twenty seventh day of September in the year of our Lord God (1637) I John Haggas of Whitby in the Diocese of York, Mason, being sick of body, but of good & perfect Memory the Lord be praised do make and ordain this my last Will and testament in manner and form following ~ First I bequeath my soul to God my maker & to Jesus Christ my Redeemer And my body to be buried where it shall please God to appoint.

Imprimis I give and bequeath to Jonas Haggas the son of Lawrence Haggas deceased all my house with the appurtences thereunto belonging where I now dwell in Baxtergate in Whitby and to his heirs for ever And also I give and bequeath unto him one quarter & a sixteenth part of one Ship or Hoy called the *Welcome* of Whitby wherein now Robert Missell is Maister, & all whatsoever belongeth unto these parts, And also I give him Three pounds Nine shillings four pence halfpenny which is stock in her for that part.

Item I give unto my son Nicholas Haggas's four children, John Haggas, Thomas, Nicholas, and Ann Haggas, twenty pounds to be equally divided amongst the And I give also to Ann Haggas my son Nicholas's wife Ten pounds

Item I give unto Jane Haggas Fifty pounds.

Item I give unto Isabell Haggas Fifty pounds; And also I give unto Mary Haggas another Fifty pounds being the daughter of my son Lawrence Haggas deceased,

Item I give unto those three daughters of my son Lawrence Haggas deceased, Jane, Isabell, & Mary Haggas All their said Father's Goods and Household Stuff in the house which my wife knows what it is, & that which I paid for unto Ralph Laund of Egton being for the full part of that Child which my son Lawrence had unto Mary Carlile his last wife; to be equally divided amongst them.

Item I give unto Elizabeth Haggas which my son Lawrence had unto his last wife Forty shillings

For the residue of my Goods, not herein bequeathed my Debts being paid & I honestly carried to the Ground, My Funeral Expenses paid and discharged; I give and bequeath unto Jane my wife whom I make and ordain the sole Executrix of this this my last will and Testament. And I desire Mr. Robert Remington and John Glover of Whitby whome I put in full power and trust to be Overseers & Supervisors of this my last will and testament that it may be honestly performed & discharged In witness whereof I have set unto this my last will & testament my hand and Seal the day and year first above-written.

Sealed and Signed in the presence of Robert Remington John Glover James Harrison

The will of John Haggas shows the havoc an outbreak of plague could cause, despite Whitby's comparatively healthy situation. The son Nicholas died during the next outbreak, in 1648, leaving several small children. John's will records the start of Jonas Haggas's fortune. (RRB)

30 The oldest Whitby vessel to have been photographed, the topsail schooner *Alert*

31 A steam tug towing the hull of a newly built steamship out of the harbour

CHAPTER 7

SCHOOLS AND SCHOLARS

The Venerable Bede, writing some fifty years after the death of St Hilda, praised her skill as a teacher, and in particular as a trainer of bishops, for she trained five of the early bishops of the English Church. She was herself a scholar, used to the company of scholars, and particularly of St Aidan whose protégé she was. Little has come directly to us from that abbey, save a few artefacts of a high artistic order, and the *Life of St Gregory the Great*, by an unnamed monk of Whitby. This was of sufficient international repute for a copy to have found its way into the library of the Monastery of St Gall in Switzerland. It was from the Northumbrian Church, of which St Hilda was a luminary, that much of northern Germany was converted to Christianity, and today pilgrims reverse the journeys of the early missionaries to visit St Hilda's abbey.

One of Hilda's own protégés was Cædmon, the herdsman, possibly of British race, who is the earliest known English poet. Only one short poem can be identified with certainty, but it is known that he spent the last years of his life making the Scriptures accessible to English readers. That this should be a worthy purpose is an indicator of the importance of teaching in the early abbey, for the vernacular Bible was a concept that was lost for the many centuries between the Conquest and the Reformation, yet both the Lindisfarne Gospels and the Vespasian Psalter were glossed into Early English for native readers.

The re-founded abbey would have a vested interest in teaching, for not all of those whose piety brought them to become brethren would be literate, and there would be novices to be taught Latin, theology, reading and writing. The monastery had a scriptorium, whose only known extant output is the *Great Book of Whitby*, and a second Cartulary, now in the British Library but which would have been engaged in producing books for the abbey library and as commissions for wealthy and devout benefactors of the abbey. The list, *c*1170, of the volumes in the abbey library contains many of the standard works of the time, with Lives of the Saints, and copies of Bede's works, as well as theological treatises, and volumes of philosophy and mathematics. Sadly, we have no comparable list from the dissolution, so it is not possible to see how the library had grown. Some of the benefactions made to the abbey were specifically for learned purposes, and were often shared between the library and the Precentor, who was responsible for the music in the abbey. Music would also have to be taught, as the singing of plainsong was a particular monastic skill. The records show that there was a song school. It might have been a means of recruiting, at least in the early days of the abbey, young novices, before the practice of accepting children as 'oblates' was discontinued in the 13th century. Among the recorded books in the abbey library is the *Liber Guidonis Monachi de Musica*, or *The Book of Brother Guy about Music*.

Other skills would be needed. Each monastery had an infirmary, for the care of sick and incapacitated monks, and of guests who could afford to pay for their maintenance, either by regular donations, or by promise of substantial bequests. Whitby also had a leper hospital, and that would continue throughout the medieval period as a refuge for the sick, handicapped and needy. In addition, there was a duty of care for the town, which would involve the visitation of the sick. There would be a series of monks who held the office of Infirmarer, and who would be skilled in the use of herbal medicine. There would be a herbarium, and successive generations of assistants would have to be trained.

The commercial life of the town, save for its brief period as a free borough, was also the responsibility of the abbot, and so there would arise a need for teaching to produce literate and numerate boys to act as clerks, not only to the abbey estates, but also to the slowly growing number of tradesmen and merchants in the town. There would be scriveners, who would act as peripatetic clerks, but if a tradesman were ambitious to rise, then he would have his own sons educated.

As a commercial seaport, Whitby would struggle with the difficult problem of casting accounts, using Roman numerals, whose base was quite different from the normal counting bases of English currency or even of quantities. It is very difficult to perform accurate calculations using Roman numerals. Even the *Valor Ecclesiasticus*, on which King Henry VIII based his decision to dissolve the religious houses, was substantially in error in many cases.

After the dissolution of the abbey, many of the towns which had been dependents of great religious houses acquired schools, endowed by the perhaps conscience-stricken king, or by those who had bought, sometimes quite cheaply, the former monastery lands. This did not happen in Whitby, and Whitby has no anciently endowed Grammar School. This was a matter for comment among early publishers of directories, such as Baines's of 1822. However, this absence of a 'grammar school' may well have been a great advantage, for such foundations often had prescribed *curricula*, more suited to gentility than to the kind of navigational skills which found the seaway into the Baltic, or avoided the terrors of a lee shore. The schoolmasters who set up in Whitby were highly skilled to fulfil the demands of what became a magnet town for the training of sea-officers.

An Act of 1511 had formalised the supervisory role of the medieval church in education, by making it compulsory for each diocese to license schoolmasters. In practice, the Act also brought surgeons and midwives under the same control. The Church was little involved with what were called petty schools, but took much more interest in any that purported to be Grammar Schools. A master who wished to set up such a 'Grammar school' must have himself nominated to the Diocesan Bishop - in the case of Whitby the Archbishop of York - as a fit person to hold office, and to instruct the young in religious matters. A few of these nominations survive, and it is clear that there was a continuous line of teaching throughout the 17th and 18th centuries until the use of the Act lapsed after 1835. There was additional pressure after the Test Act of 1673 when schoolmasters had to swear that they were not non-conformists, and not, therefore, banned from holding public office. Any schoolmaster who was not so licensed was liable to 'presentment' at the Church courts, as was any clergyman who eked out his income by unlicensed teaching.

In the late 17th century increases in Whitby's prosperity there must have been growth in the number of educational opportunities, for all Whitby's economic involvements required expertise, particularly in mathematics. Mining and manufacturing, as for alum, involved skill in surveying, as well as chemistry, and navigation is a mathematical art. So too was the developing technology of ship-building. In one year alone three schoolmasters were given certificates of approbation, James Moxon, George Barker and George Ward, and there were two others at least flourishing in the town, one of them a graduate.

Many men taught without any licence at all, so that it is only in other documents such as parish registers, and probate entries that one learns of their names. Baines's *Directory of Yorkshire* of 1822 records several private schools, as well as the flourishing Free schools. Lionel Charlton, an extraordinary polymath, whose *History of Whitby* (1778) is still consulted for its translations of the early charters of the abbey, described himself as a surveyor and teacher of mathematics, and earned his livelihood at both professions. At the time when Charlton was teaching mathematics Whitby was in its most prolific period in output from its shipyards, and in registration of ships and thus employment of mariners.

The mariners, the skilled and trained men who became the sea officers, needed to learn mathematics, and had to be literate enough to keep ships' logs and ships' books, in which were recorded the financial transactions of each voyage. The extant logs reveal not only neatness of hand, and accuracy in navigation, but at times a literary flow which enlivens what is otherwise dull work. Thomas Etty, aged 20, keeping the journal of the *George* during the long hard winter of 1800-1801 ashore in Russia, shows a dry humour. He spent two years at the Bluecoat School in York, where he was born, but as an apprentice to John Chapman would have spent his winters in study and schooling. There is extant the navigation exercise book which Henry Simpson used in 1711, as well as textbooks on rigging, ship design and other seafaring crafts. William Scoresby junior first went to sea with his father at the age of ten, but he also attended the University of Edinburgh before himself becoming master of a whaling ship at the age of twenty-three.

It is not until the 19th century that the existence of schools is systematically recorded. During the great wave of enthusiasm for education, particularly for the children of the poor, so that they might be fitted to earn a living and thus escape from the poverty trap, there was pressure from within church circles for the foundation of free schools.

The impetus in Whitby came from the Lancasterian movement, a group influenced by Joseph Lancaster, a Quaker. In 1808 the Royal Lancasterian Society was founded to establish schools, and to carry out Lancaster's ideas, among which was the use of monitors to assist with the dissemination of knowledge. Lancaster left the Society two years later, but although the name was changed to the *British and Foreign School Society* the ideas persisted, and the original name is perpetuated on the charity boards which list the generous donations from the benefactors who supported the schools, particularly the one for girls, which was founded shortly after the public school for boys. In a town where a substantial proportion of the male population was at sea for much of the year, it was essential that girls should be literate and numerate to keep the business life of the town going. Both schools were in use until the 1960s, brought under the wing of the local authority. One, which narrowly escaped destruction by a bomb in the 1939-45 war, has since been demolished, and the other is now closed, though its buildings are still in use.

It is significant that the Presbyterian minister who was Whitby's second historian, George Young, should speak so highly in 1817 of the work both schools were doing. The lists of 'scholars' in the 1851 Census speaks well of the use to which the schools were put. In due course they were joined by church schools of other denominations, and after 1870 by board schools, and in 1912 by Whitby County School, later Whitby Grammar School, then Whitby School, and now Whitby Community College. Today there are two middle schools, Caedmon and Eskdale, and four community primary schools, with the Roman Catholic Church retaining its church school. At the same time, independent education continued, running the gamut of dame schools to independent 'academies' with various grandiose names. Sneaton Castle has housed several, starting in 1813 with one run by Revd J. T. Holloway. Later the building was extended, in private hands, to resemble a castle, and in 1914 was set to become a preparatory school. However, war recalled the principal to the colours, and it was then leased, and later bought, by the fledgling Order of the Holy Paraclete as a priory and girls' school, which also trained teachers. The school closed in 1997, and the Order now runs a successful study centre. The sometime 'Hildathorpe College' has also gone, but St Hilda is commemorated as a teacher by the priory that bears her name, and in the Roman Catholic primary school.

There have always been, and still are, in any town individual teachers of specialist subjects, catering not for the vocational skills needed by engineers or navigators, but for the cultural activities of a prospering elite, and aspiring middle class. From time to time references are found in registers and probate documents to dancing-masters and teachers of drawing. One such was John Bird, apprenticed in his youth to a house-painter, and then, alongside his career as an artist and teacher of drawing, the first Keeper of the Whitby Museum, founded in 1823.

Music teachers, particularly those teaching singing and pianoforte, doubled as church organists and accompanists and performers at *soirées*. Most of them led blameless, uneventful lives, though being associated with the New Chapel in Baxtergate seems to have been a little hazardous. There, in the earlier part of the 19th century the services of one Mr Newby Duck were obtained to lead the music. He led a band of Singing Girls, all paid a modest honorarium, until the proprietors found themselves a little short of funds, and decided to cut the honorarium. The girls took offence, and resigned, so the proprietors decided to manage with the musical leadership of the Chapel Clerk. A year of his singing seems to have been sufficient for their nerves, for at the next annual meeting Mr Duck and the girls were re-instated at the original fee.

The same establishment parted company in 1828 with another organist, under much more dubious circumstances, which are recorded only in the letters of protest received from the organist herself, who explained that the 'gossip' had arisen only because of jealousy, and that a certain gentleman was in the habit of calling on her solely for the purpose of having pianoforte lessons. The proprietors were apparently not impressed, and in another letter her brother offered to collect her music books from the chapel at a certain time. Nonetheless, a tradition of music persisted, and Whitby has a fine collection of church organs, and a long tradition of amateur opera, of music festivals, and male-voice and other choirs.

Whitby had theatres, one in the Paddock, opened in 1763, and one opened in Scate Lane, now Brunswick Street, in 1784, and burnt down in 1823. That may well have staged the plays of Francis Gibson, Collector of Customs, the edition of one of whose plays, *Streonshall Abbey*, has a frontispiece by Thomas Bewicke.

CHAPTER 8

ARTISTS, GEOLOGISTS AND LADY NOVELISTS

Whitby's most dominant feature is the ruin of the church of the medieval abbey, and the one of the most impressive aspects of that is the beauty of its stone-masonry. The brindled stone from Aislaby quarry has been fashioned and carved with delicacy and skill which has withstood seven centuries of wind and salt. There are Early English lancets, Decorated window traceries and the delicate rose window of the north transept. There are heads and figures high above the congregation, and there is the superlative east wall of the choir. Sadly, though we know the name of the architect who planned the first abbey church after the refoundation, a man called Godfrey, we do not yet know the names of the men who created the final masterpiece.

Much of the stonework of the abbey has been lost, but in walls in other places in the town are to be seen individual stones of great beauty. Much was re-used in Abbey House, one of whose garden walls has a strange collection of random decorated stonework. The same skill is to be seen, hidden now by the 17th century Cholmley pew, in the fine Norman arch-work of the parish church, but the rest of the parish church is a homely square vernacular building, much enlarged and altered to enclose its growing family, by members of that family, and rather large and cumbersome now that the family has grown and gone.

Even the tablets of improving texts are endearingly domestic, done, no doubt, by a local sign-writer, probably in the late 17th century. Sometimes these individuals are known to us, from accounts kept by churchwardens and treasurers. We know, for instance, that Valentine Plowright gilded the "captiles" - he was no scholar - of the coopered pillars in the New Chapel in Baxtergate. Often men who became well-known and respected as artists and teachers of art began their careers in more prosaïc employments, like those of John Bird and George Chambers, who were respectively trained as house and stage-scenery painters.

In common with many flourishing northern towns, Whitby had a Mechanics' Institute, founded in 1845, and a Subscription Library. There was also an ambitious project, devised by Revd George Young, to establish a Botanic Garden in 1812, and a list of its plants survives in the museum. In 1823, a time which saw many such organisations founded in the north, there was established the Whitby Literary and Philosophical Society. Under its auspices grew Whitby Museum, now in Pannett Park, but from 1827 on the second floor of a building shared with the Subscription Library and the Public Baths beside the harbour. The men and women who have served the museum in unpaid capacities have raised it to pre-eminence among small regional museums.

It has a reputation for geology, based on the work of one of its earliest keepers, Martin Simpson, which makes it a regular venue for film work about fossils. Its fossil collection, ranging from tiny ammonites, for centuries a symbol of St Hilda's Whitby because of a legend of her banishment of the snakes, to a complete ichthyosaurus, is one of the best in the north of England. Now, with the aid of the Heritage Lottery Fund, it has a new state-of-the art extension to house a costume gallery, working areas, lecture hall and exhibition space. Generations of seafarers have brought curiosities from overseas, as well as paintings and models of ships, and an excellent collection of shipping papers. All this has been freely available to members, and to residents of the town, for over 150 years. There have been monthly lectures, symposia and *conversazioni,* as fashions have passed, but the Museum's uniqueness lies in the gifted amateur keepers and curators who still manage the museum and library, and deal with international queries. Computerisation has brought it into a third century, as a registered museum, but its particular quality lies in its continuity of effort, and great dedication to Whitby and its history and influence. The list of early presidents of the Society includes Robert Stephenson, the railway engineer, whose father George Stephenson, the pioneer of railways, designed the Pickering to Whitby railway which was opened in 1836.

From the end of the 18th century Whitby became a favoured resort of artists drawn by its setting and its 'romantic' ruins. A further attraction, it must be said, was the prosperity which enabled dedications to be made to the famous and the wealthy, and which provided a source of commissions for portraits, and for paintings of sailing vessels. Many of the wealthy merchants and ship-owners who supported Whitby's greatest period of economic prosperity were painted by respected portrait artists of their day, and the originals, or engravings taken from them, hang in the

Museum. It is one of the joys of history in Whitby that it is possible to put faces to some at least of the names which recur in historical record, and even to see family likeness as the elite groups intermarried.

An early artist of repute who painted Whitby faces was Sir Godfrey Kneller, one of whose attributed portraits, of Peregrine Lascelles, hangs in the Museum. J. M. W. Turner painted here, as did Samuel Prout and Algernon Newton, J. P. Neale and David Wilkie, and many of their paintings were reproduced by competent Whitby engravers whose work is now in the Museum, and which was published in a collected edition by the late Dr. Thomas English in 1923. There are fine marine paintings, both of seascapes and of ships, many of them by the Whitby-born George, Richard and Mary Weatherill, and humbler, but no less engaging 'pierhead' paintings of ships, created by local house-painters in distant ports. The Pannett Art Gallery, endowed by a bequest from Alderman Robert Pannett, and opened in 1931, contains a fine collection of paintings, particularly by George, Richard and Mary Weatherill, and acts as host to visiting exhibitions.

It is not only trade, the sea and the abbey ruins that have brought fame to Whitby, for since the middle of the 19th century it has been a centre for the study of geology, and particularly of fossils, in which it abounds. Its early pre-eminence in this field is largely due to the work of one of the earliest curators of the Museum, Martin Simpson, born in 1800 in the village of Stainsacre, and apprenticed to a cabinet-maker by his master-mariner father, who died when Martin was sixteen. Martin Simpson subsequently studied, as did others of his generation in Whitby, at the University of Edinburgh, and by 1824 he was teaching and lecturing in the West Riding. It has to be remembered that he was an older contemporary of Charles Darwin (1809-1882) and Robert FitzRoy (1805-1864), from whose voyage in HMS *Beagle* came new geological observations.

Simpson returned to Whitby in 1837, and was appointed keeper of the museum. Although lack of funds drove him to seek other sources of income, his life's work was the scientific description and naming of the fossils found in the *lias* shales of the Yorkshire Coast; a recent president of the Whitby Literary and Philosophical Society, Professor J. E. Hemingway, FRS, described him as a foremost authority on the ammonite fossils. He published greatly respected scientific treatises on fossils, subsidising them with more popular guidebooks, and his personal collection is one of the most precious assets of the museum. Simpson's work has inspired and attracted geologists ever since, and the sight of groups of students with hard hats and little hammers is very common. Visitors have been known to quarry the churchyard wall for fossils, a practice discouraged by the hard-pressed churchwardens! It means also that the souvenir shops offer things of greater age than are available in most seaside resorts, as visitors purchase split and polished ammonites, which are mounted as trophies.

More famous still is the jet which has been carved since Roman times, but which came to particular pre-eminence in the time of mourning for Prince Albert, who died in 1861. Jet is chiefly found in the cliffs, though some was mined in the moors, and at its peak the jet industry employed over 1,000 men. Much of the output of the jet workshops was in the form of mourning jewellery, often very elaborately and intricately carved, sometimes in relief, and using the initials *I M O* (in memory of) as a motif. Some of the mourning sets, of earrings, brooches and necklaces, were heavy and ornate, and were very laborious to create. Much, of course, was for the lower-market trade, so that there was a wide range of skills, but some of the finest carvings are of extreme beauty, and won many prizes internationally. Included among these is a pair of medallions of Emperor Napoleon III and Empress Eugenie of France, by Charles Bryan, which won first prize at the Paris Exhibition of 1867. They are particularly prized because they are carved from single pieces of jet. Jet was rarely found in large pieces, and much of the output of the workshops was in the form of very small items. However, models, individual communion cups and knife handles were among objects carved from the larger pieces. There are still jet carvers in Whitby, and it is possible to buy antique jet jewellery in the town, but the industry, being, sadly, founded on fashion, suffered great distress and poverty when fashions changed and other kinds of costume jewellery took the place of jet. Many of the men who carved the jet were neat-fingered journeymen craftsmen, but among them were artists of great skill and flair.

Another artist who was greatly concerned about the jet workers, particularly after the slump, was Mary Linskill, Whitby born and bred, whose novels of life in 19th century Whitby draw largely on her own experiences. She is no longer fashionable, yet the titles she gave her books, and some of her descriptions, live on in the collective memory of the people of Whitby. Whitby is indeed the *Haven Under the Hill*, and that title was taken by the pioneering photographer, Frank Meadow Sutcliffe, most of whose working life was spent in Whitby, for what is one of his most famous photographs, of Whitby taken from the 199 Church Stairs looking down over the smoking chimneys of the town. Mary died relatively young, a victim of tuberculosis, which was not uncommon in the densely populated old town where she lived. In later years another Whitby woman achieved fame as a novelist, Storm Jameson, the centenary of whose birth fell in 1989. Her books are more widely read and are still in print, and her life took her away from Whitby, while Mary Linskill stayed within its bounds. Other writers came to Whitby and felt its influence. Of these, three are well remembered, Lewis Carroll and Bram Stoker, and Elizabeth Gaskell, one of the great women novelists of the 19th century.

Lewis Carroll came to Whitby as a summer visitor at the time when it was a fashionable watering place for the intelligentsia. It is easy to look at the long strand which gave its name to the Liberty of the abbey, and think that it was the inspiration for the *Walrus and the Carpenter*, or the *Lobster Quadrille*, or imagine that half-remembered tales of the mad, and murderous, Russian Tsar Paul I, whose shadow fell over the seafaring community of Whitby in 1800, suggested the Red Queen. Bram Stoker, whose best-known work of fiction led to countless horror films, wrote *Dracula* while visiting Whitby, setting part of it in the town. His description of the east cliff and St Mary's churchyard are evocative, even if one would wish his book had become less of a cult. It becomes difficult to convince some enthusiasts that *Dracula* really was fiction.

Perhaps the most enduring of all the writers who have taken Whitby as a subject is Elizabeth Gaskell, who came, like Carroll, as a summer visitor, but who captured the atmosphere of 18th century Whitby in her novel *Sylvia's Lovers*, set in Whitby during the days of the whale fishery and the French Wars. She took the incident of the pressgang riot of 1793, and wrote of the effects on the community of war, whaling and civil strife. Her novel encapsulates the stress on the people who lived through those events, and although she spent only a few weeks in Whitby, her perception and comprehension of the nature of the town, and her grasp of its experiences, are remarkable.

32 A romantic view of two brigs on their mud berths

33 A view from the west cliff

34 Selling the catch in the days before the fish-market building was erected on the quay

35 Whitby in the 19th century, showing the railway station, centre left

CHAPTER 9

HOUSES AND PEOPLE OF GOD

For its population (now about 13,500), Whitby probably has had more churches and other places of worship than most towns of comparable size. There are now three Anglican churches, St Mary's parish church, St Hilda's, and St John's, together with the Anglican St Hilda's Priory and a Seamen's Mission. There is a Roman Catholic church, and a small Roman Catholic convent. The Society of Friends, once a leading group in 18th century Whitby, with an extra-ordinary influence in the trading practices of the port, has recently sold its meeting-house in Church Street; the Methodist Church has had over time five churches. In Flowergate there are two more churches, the United Reformed and the old Unitarian chapel, and there is a separate Congregational church in Skinner Street; Jehovah's Witnesses have a Kingdom Hall. The 'New Chapel' in Baxtergate, once the Anglican proprietary chapel of St Ninian, has now seceded into independence. More recent arrivals are the Evangelical Church and the New Life Church. Gone, replaced or put to other uses are many more; St Michael's Church, a chapel of ease in Church Street; the old 'iron' church which was replaced by St Hilda's; the medieval chapel replaced by St Ninian's; the Scots Presbyterian church of which the historian George Young was minister, and the Salvation Army citadel. Most notable of all is the roofless church of the abbey, still used from time to time for out-door services.

Over the years there would have been other, temporary buildings, lost because replaced, or because fashions in religion change as in every other sphere. Before the non-conformist churches acquired the freedom to worship which is now their right, licences had to be obtained for the use of meeting-rooms, often in private houses, for their congregations, and the diocesan and county archives hold collections of licences for private meeting houses whose identity is now lost. Other congregations met in danger and secrecy in the times of persecution, and it was within the parish of Whitby, at Littlebeck, in 1678, that the priest, Father Nicholas Postgate, over eighty years old, was captured, and later hanged, drawn and quartered at York. For over forty years he had acted as a priest to the beleaguered Catholic population of the area.

Quakers, too, were persecuted, both by the established church, usually for non-attendance at church services, and for refusal to pay church rates, but also by the unthinking mob, who attacked their business premises and harassed their members. George Fox himself, about 1654, visited Whitby and the Society of Friends he founded produced many of the most successful and upright merchants, ship-builders and ship-owners of the 18th and 19th century, including John Walker, to whom James Cook was apprenticed. They were bankers as well, Simpsons, Chapmans, Saunders and others, much respected for their probity, and it is one of these families that Elizabeth Gaskell, herself the wife of a Unitarian Minister, described in *Sylvia's Lovers*. Their rigorous views on the evil of war led to conflict among their own brethren, and during the wars of the 18th century, when French privateers greatly increased the hazards to shipping, members of the Society had to choose between arming their ships for defence, and solemn rejection by the Society.

John Wesley oversaw the establishment of Methodist congregations in Whitby, visiting them annually, and himself suffering persecution. On one occasion, when he began to preach to his out-door congregation on the Church Stairs, the bell-ringers of the parish church set out to drown his preaching, by ringing the bells. They failed, and he completed his sermon, and in 1988, when the 250th anniversary of Wesley's conversion was celebrated by the Methodist Church, an exhibition in his honour was mounted in the parish church, and the ringers rang a full peal of 5,000 changes in penitence for their predecessors' actions.

Not all of Whitby despised the new 'Methodists', for Lionel Charlton wrote in his *History* of his great respect for the godly work which was being done by the Methodists in the town, particularly among the poor and un-churched. Indeed it was from the non-conformist churches that the first public education became available for poor children in Whitby, with the foundation of the Lancasterian Schools, and the list of Anglican donors to the public subscription indicates a good measure of acceptance of their outlook. It was from the Scots Presbyterian Revd George Young that much of the concept of self-help and intellectual curiosity came that led to developments such as the botanical garden and the museum.

But Whitby's existence owed most to the 'established' Church of its time. Although St Hilda had been much influenced by the great Celtic saint, Aidan, the links forged at the Synod of Whitby of 664 led England closer to Europe, and the re-foundation of the abbey in 1078 was as a Benedictine house, whose later abbots played their part in national affairs. Yet it was the 'establishment' itself, in the person of King Henry VIII, that destroyed the medieval abbey, but left behind an awareness of the importance of religion which must stem from the precariousness of life whose existence depended on the mercurial nature of the North Sea.

There was a need for theological exactitude, and a polarisation of views on the nature of God, which seems to have led to a determination to belong overtly to one part or another of the Church. It is not an easy thing to risk the penalties which awaited Father Nicholas Postgate, or to face the derision of the mob, or the denial of civic rights which was the fate of any citizen who failed to comply with the Test Act. The lists of schoolmasters who had to subscribe to that Act in the late 17th century in order to earn a living is a witness to that. There were heavy fines for Roman Catholic recusants for failing to attend church, but also for Quakers and 'Dissenters'.

And for the conforming Anglican, of course, there was the civic duty which might fall to his lot, unasked, of being Churchwarden, Overseer of the Poor, or Highway Surveyor, as elected by the Easter Vestry. Generally such a task fell to those who could afford it, and they then had to levy and collect the 'cess' or rates which paid for the upkeep of the church and churchyard, for paving the streets and for maintaining the poor of the town. As economic stress affected the town from time to time, due to weather, disease or war, those rates would be hard to collect. There were many who paid selectively, or not at all, because of religious scruple, yet those same men and women who refused to pay would be the business and trade partners of those who collected. Among the defaulters listed in rate books, and in 'presentations', or indictments, at the Church Courts, are many of the wealthiest men and women in Whitby, withholding church rates on religious grounds, Chapmans, Simpsons, Barricks, Haggases and Meggisons. Even the Cholmleys, lords of the manor, were for a time Catholic recusants in the late 16th and early 17th centuries, giving refuge in their house on the east cliff to the seminary priests sent from the continent to aid the Catholic population. Their allegiance cost them dearly, in fines, and in the case of Mrs Margaret Cholmley, in imprisonment, but around 1603-4 they conformed to the Church of England.

The Quakers found a way to compensate for their unwillingness to pay towards the upkeep of the parish church whose vestry ran the town.

Badly needed harbour and other public works in the town were enabled by private Acts of Parliament, which levied statutory rather than church rates, and Quakers willingly paid those, and often acted as Trustees for such works.

The townscape of Whitby is dominated by the buildings erected by these various groupings, as people gradually moved from the populous lower streets of the 'old town' to the newer 'suburbs'. Much of the building is Victorian Gothic, in the Anglican St Hilda's and its Catholic namesake, in St John's, and in the former Brunswick Methodist Church and the West Cliff Congregational Church. There are delightful meeting-houses of an earlier style, for Unitarians and Quakers, and there are chapels in buildings designed for other purposes, such as the Seamen's Mission chapel in the former Haggersgate House, and the Evangelical Church in a former shop in Skinner Street. There are shops, too, in former chapels, such as the Wesleyan Methodist Church in Church Street, but the building which most reflects the uniqueness of Whitby's ecclesiastical life must be St Mary's parish church.

The present parish church building was begun in 1110, but was probably built on the foundations of an earlier church, possibly that belonging to St Hilda's abbey. It is known that members of the Northumbrian royal house were buried there. It would initially have been a timber church, and some remains of wattle and daub have been found, though a later stone church would possibly have been built.

There is some Norman stonework in St Mary's, including a good Norman chancel, though that is obscured to a large extent by the early 17th century pew erected by the Cholmley family. There are similarly obscured Norman windows in the south wall. At first there would be simply a nave and a chancel, to provide for people and for priest, staffed by a priest from among the monks. The building itself reflects all the history of Whitby's development. A tower was added around 1170, some forty years after the town began to develop as a burgage. A few years after King John had rescinded the charter of incorporation, a north transept was added. By then the town was trading busily in salt herrings, wool and other commodities, and the church would have expanded to accommodate the rising merchant class, and their visitors from overseas. Towards the end of the 14th century a second transept was built, to make the church cruciform. This was the time when surviving abbey accounts show a town of some prosperity, which had built quays and a bridge, and whose wills reveal flourishing guilds, as well as altars to various saints within the parish church. There were probably no pews in the pre-reformation church, with only the infirm seated, on a ledge round the wall, such as may be seen in the abbey church. That, of course, assumes that the infirm managed to climb the stairs from the town.

The earliest pews are of 17th century origin, and include the ornate Cholmley pew, standing on its corkscrew pillars and dominating the whole as the Cholmleys were to dominate the town for several centuries. There are other pews, however, as the prosperous citizens desired to seat themselves in accordance with the new ways of the church. Gradually, as the congregation expanded and became wealthier, so the pews became more elaborate, other private pews appeared, either bought or rented, and the church began to take on its now familiar appearance. At the time its interior would have been like that of other 18th century churches, in which the wealthy could seat themselves apart from the poor. Gradually, as Whitby prospered, galleries were built to take the surplus population and provide for growing prosperity.

In 1818 the north transept was removed and the cruciform shape, no longer important to a congregation for whom worship had abandoned much of its sacramental nature, was lost. The building was virtually squared to allow for many more pews and galleries. This building project provided desperately-needed work for seamen and soldiers cast ashore after the end of the Napoleonic wars. The three-decker pulpit had already been added, for preaching was the most important aspect of worship at this stage, and the church, with the flat, vernacular roof built earlier by ships' carpenters, became the extra-ordinary structure which it is today. It seats 1,500 people, and that says much for the church-going habits of the early 19th century, though, many of the congregation would be 'pressed' rather than voluntary, and the church was probably rarely full. The graffiti of ships carved out of sight in the pews by bored apprentices over many years is testimony to this, and yet at the same time there were congregations of Quakers, Methodists, Presbyterians, Catholics and others, all gathered on Sunday to worship God.

There was another Anglican church in the town, built in 1778, reflecting in other ways Whitby's independence of mind. Its very existence was part of the process of preservation which has kept St Mary's in its early 19th century form, for it was the church building on the west side and in the lower part of the town which meant that St Mary's escaped the great refurbishments and 'restorations' of the late Victorian period. By then the fashionable and more accessible churches were the newer ones, and there was probably no more incentive to rebuild St Mary's, so Whitby has a rare example of an unaltered church from a lost period of churchmanship. In 1778, however, the citizens of Whitby were not happy with the state of the church, particularly the Anglican church, for St Mary's was difficult of access, and the only chapel of ease, St Ninian's, was damp and did not reflect the growing economic strength of the town. The endowments of the parish church were in the hands of the Archbishop, and successive petitions had failed to stir him, or his predecessors, to do anything to help. Whitby's entrepreneurs took matters into their own hands, and provided their own New Chapel, its ownership held in shares, like a ship.

The building, no longer Anglican, is much as when it was built, save for renewed pews from the late 19th century, a rather charming example of 18th century vernacular church architecture. It is built outwardly of the brick which was fashionable in the better houses of the time, with a slate roof, brought overland from Hull at great expense because the War of American Independence made shipping dangerous, and with a wealth of timber provided and fashioned by the same men who built the great ships for Cook and the Scoresbys. William Scoresby junior was himself called to become a priest under the influence of the minister of the new chapel in his day, Revd Doctor Holloway. It is a Whitby church, unique as Whitby is, and mirroring its achievements, as does in a different way St Mary's. Rather later, the other Anglican churches were built in the town, St Michael's, on Church Street, now demolished, St John's at the end of Baxtergate, and the large cathedral-like St Hilda's which dominates the west cliff. Whitby was founded by the church, and it is its church buildings which are its greatest memorials, for they reflect its own awareness of its identity as St Hilda's town, and yet of its skill as ship-builders and seafarers, and entrepreneurs. Now its churches act as seamarks for ships, and magnets for the many thousands of visitors who come to the town, pilgrims in fact if not in intention, to one of the cradles of English Christianity.

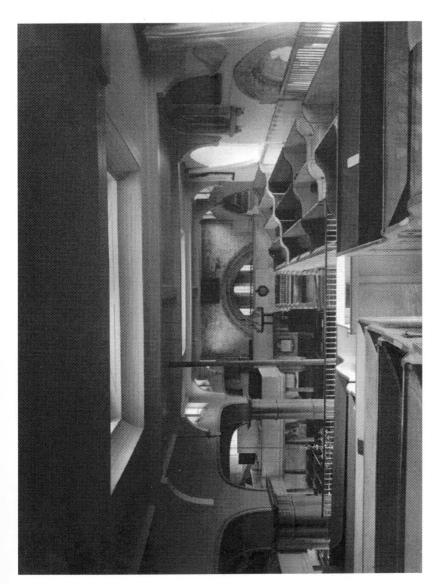

36 The interior of St Mary's Church

37 The handsome Victorian reredos in St Hilda's Church

CHAPTER 10

EPILOGUE

Whitby in the early 21st century would still be recognisable to many of its past inhabitants. They might marvel at the development on the west cliff; they would certainly approve of the drainage, and of the surfaced roads, and rejoice in the street lighting. Even George Young, writing in 1817, complained that there was no street lighting provided by the parish. They might find the demolition of the warehouses which once lined the harbour side of Church Street a strange waste of good burgage land, and they would wonder at the loss of the galleried cottages which climbed the cliffs behind Church Street. They would certainly admire the piers, and be impressed by the diligence and efficiency of the dredger which keeps clear the channels in the harbour for the now sadly occasional commercial shipping. The alum mines have been replaced by potash, though this rarely forms part of the harbour trade, and the fish is cod, haddock and shell-fish rather than the Greenland whale or the 'silver darlings' of the great days of the herring fishery. The lifeboat station is still there, recently re-built and has two boats, for both deep water and inshore work, and the lifeboats of the past, including the last rowing lifeboat to be taken out of service, are recorded in the lifeboat museum.

Whitby Rock is still treacherous, and claims its victims, though less often, and then generally recreational sailors, though from time to time the North Sea reminds its fishermen that they should not take it for granted. On the far horizon, where whaling ships, collier brigs and Baltic traders were watched for, there are now deep-water tankers heading for the Tees. Until recently the only sails in Whitby were on the dinghies and yachts which moor at the marina. However the visits of tall ships such as the replica of HM Bark *Endeavour*, which carried James Cook, Whitby-trained, on his first great voyage of discovery, have given people a glimpse of what the townscape of Whitby would have been like when even part of its late 18th century fleet of over 300 sailing vessels was in the harbour. The top of *Endeavour's* mainmast was level with St Mary's churchyard.

38 Whitby in 2007 from the high-level bridge over the Esk

39 Young people from around the world visit Whitby for its history

40 Church Street is popular with Whitby's tourists

41 Whitby dry-dock, ship-yard and marina

Families which produced generations of master mariners have lost all but a nostalgic connection with the sea, as the merchant fleet has contracted. The families from the fishing community are now quite likely to be living on new estates rather than in the yards close to the harbour side, and fishing is a high technology industry now, with an industry-led fisheries school appropriately placed on the top floor of the Seamen's Mission.

On the east cliff still stand the ruins of the abbey, neat and dignified in the care of English Heritage, and the square shape of St Mary's Church, visited by over 120,000 people every year. The bells ring for Thursday practice and Sunday service, and bring the old year out and the new year in as they have done for centuries.

Yet to write thus is to wallow in nostalgia, and Whitby has never wallowed. Its presence in the face of so much trial from the sea, the wind, the Danes, the Conqueror, the Norwegians, the Scots, the Dutch, the French, the Americans, the Russians and the Germans, all in turn, and interspersed with economic change and stress, indicates its determination and its resilience, and perhaps most of all the strength of its people, and particularly of its women. The community founded by that formidable lady from the 7th century has produced successive generations of women who could cope with the business, as well as the domestic problems of fatherless homes, while men went to sea, and who could hold the family together, often under conditions of extreme stress.

Now, there is the fishing industry, which still takes men to sea, and the commercial port and marina, and there is the industrial estate. Moreover, there are tourists, from all over the world, in search of many different aspects of this community. Some seek for religious enlightenment in the steps of St Hilda; some follow Cook and the Scoresbys, or seek ancestors among the wandering seafarers of the 18th and 19th century. Many enjoy the sands which so impressed the 19th century visitors, while others wander through the old town and along the harbour, seeing it all as 'quaint', and rather old-fashioned. There is nothing 'high-rise' in Whitby, as the late Alec Clifton-Taylor observed. Few go away disappointed. Whitby is a town with a surprising ability to grip the imagination. Most towns of Whitby's size have limited horizons and spheres of influence, providing markets and services for neighbouring agricultural areas, and with at best a single historic figure, perhaps a London merchant, or an inventor, or a Tudor playwright.

Whitby's horizons are the four corners of the earth. She is twinned with Whitby in Ontario, with Port Stanley in the Falklands, with

Anchorage in Alaska, with Cooktown in Queensland and with Tonga. Those are places discovered by Cook, or visited by him, but they and many other places were visited by Whitby-built ships, in the First Fleet seeking scurvy grass in the Falklands, as East Indiamen rounding the Cape of Good Hope, or carrying emigrants from the great depressions of the early 19th century to Quebec. There was a settlement at Tangier in Morocco called Whitby, when Sir Hugh Cholmley, a contemporary of Samuel Pepys, was Surveyor-General there. Whitby ships sailed as far as possible north into the Arctic, and close to the great continent of Antarctica. Australia and New Zealand owe their recent history to the great enabling voyages of exploration undertaken in a Whitby collier chosen because of its sturdy strength and ability to survive all weathers. Northern Germany was converted to Christianity by men trained or influenced by St Hilda, and we owe our way of calculating the dates of the great moveable feasts of the church, and much else besides, to a decision to join Europe, taken not in the 20th century, but in the 7th, when King Oswy gave his casting vote to St Peter and Rome, rather than to the Celtic church.

This book is a series of snapshots of aspects of a town, for how else could one possibly compress 1,300 years of important events and people into some 28,000 words? It cannot be comprehensive, for Whitby has generated a more complex record of achievement than many cities twenty times its size. It has left its mark on both hemispheres, and even in outer space. *Endeavour* set out to record the Transit of Venus in 1768, and landed on the moon in 1974. Whitby brought England closer to Europe, and helped to found today's Commonwealth. Whitby is an extraordinary town.

FURTHER READING

Readers may like to read further into Whitby's history.

Barker, R. R., *Prisoners of the Tsar; East Coast Sailors Held in Russia, 1800-1801*, Highgate Publications, 1992

Barker, R. R., *The Whitby Sisters*, Order of the Holy Paraclete, 2001

Barrow, T., *The Whaling Trade of North-East England, 1750-1850*, University of Sunderland Press, 2001

Gaskin, R. T., *The Old Seaport of Whitby*, first published, Forth, Whitby, 1909, Caedmon reprints, 1986

Labistour, P., *A Rum Do, Smuggling in and Around Robin Hood's Bay*, Marine Arts Publications, 1996

Lewis, D. B., (ed.) *The Yorkshire Coast*, Normandy Press, 1991

Weatherill, R., *The Ancient Port of Whitby and its Shipping*, Horne, Whitby, 1908

Frank, P. *Yorkshire Fisherfolk*, Phillimore, 2002.

Bell, G. *The Whitby and Pickering to Scarborough Railway*, Blackthorn Press, 2008

Robinson, R. *A History of the Yorkshire Coast Fishing Industry*, Hull University Press, 1987

INDEX

Abbey   vi, 8, 93
abbey church   18
Abbey House   84
Abbey plain   viii
Abbey Pond   vi
Abbot of Whitby   13, 60
Ælfleda   5, 58
Aidan   4
Aislaby quarry   84
Alaska   107
Allanson, Isaac   26
alum   viii, 27, 40, 69, 72
Anchorage   107
Angel Hotel   48
Angles   4
Anglican churches   93
Anglo Saxon Chronicle   5, 6
anti-aircraft batteries   64
Archbishop of York   80
Arctic   44
Argument's Yard   vi, 23
artists   86
Ascension Eve   30
Australia   44, 61, 62, 107

backstaff   41
Bagdale Beck   29
Bagwith, Christopher   25
Baine's Directory of Yorkshire   80
Baltic   27, 43, 72, 80
banking   73, 94
Barker, William   27
Barry, Thomas   42, 70
Battery Parade   64
Battle of Copenhagen   63

Battle of the Standard   59
Baxtergate   24, 29, 48, 69, 82, 84, 93, 98
Bayeux Tapestry   12
Bede   3, 5, 78
Bell Island   26
Benedictine   14, 18
Bernicia   4
Berwick   41, 60
Bewicke, Thomas   83
Bird, John   82, 84
Bishop of Carlisle   13
Black Nab   viii, 52
blockade   40
Blome, Richard   24
blubber-houses   28
Bluecoat School   81
bombardment   14
Bordeaux   41, 47
Borders   59
Bosa, Bishop of York   5
Boston   46
botanical garden   94
Botany Bay   26, 46, 62
Bradford   44
bridge   17, 24, 25, 36, 64
British and Foreign School Soc   81
Broomfield Terrace   29
Brown, Elizabeth   69
Brown, Jonas   69
Bruce, Robert the   59
Brunswick Methodist Church   96
Brus, de of Annandale   59
Brus, Peter de   13, 59
Bryan, Charles   87
burgage plots   15, 16

Burgess Pier	vi, 29	cold war	64
Burgesses	17, 24	Collector of Customs	71
Bushell, Browne	48	collier brigs	101
		Columba	4
Cædmon	5, 78	Commonwealth	57
Campion, Mrs Margaret	69	Company of New England	25
Campions' Bank	69	compass	41
Cape Horn	26	Congregational church	93
Carlile, Mary	75	Consistory Court	45
Carlisle	59	contraband	45
Carroll, Lewis	88	Conyers, Gregory	18
Cartulary	7, 11, 12, 78	Conyers, John	14
Catherine the Great	69	Cook, James Capt	26, 43, 46,
Catholics	97		68, 94, 101
Catts	43		106
Census	69, 74	Cooktown	107
Chambers, George	84	County School	64
Chandlery	47	Crosseby	59
Chapman, John	81	crow's nest	44
charity boards	73	Customs Port of Whitby	24
Charles I, King	16, 61		
Charles Stuart, Prince	62	Dacre, Robert de	14
Charlton, Lionel	vi, xi, 18, 43,	Danby	1
	80, 81, 94	Danby castle	13
Cholmley mansion	2, 13	dancing-masters	82
Cholmley, Elizabeth	47	Danelaw	6
Cholmley, Henry	61	Darwin, Charles	86
Cholmley, Mrs Margaret	95	David I, King	59
Cholmley, Sir Hugh	61, 107	Defoe, Daniel	24, 27
Cholmleys	18, 28, 61, 96	Deira	4
Church courts	95	Denmark	4
Church St	48, 93, 101,	Dickson, Andrew	25
	104	dissolution	18
church stairs	10, 15, 87	Divall, Henry abbot	18, 60
Churchwardens	71, 87	Dock End	29
Cistercian Order	12, 14	Domesday Book	6, 7, 11,
civil wars	61	d'Orleans	17
Cleveland Hills	1	Douglas, William	45
Clifton-Taylor, Alec	106	Dracula	88
Cnut, King	6	drawbridge	25, 35
Coal	17, 27	Duck, Newby	82, 83
Cock Beck	29	Dunkirk	47
Cock Mill	28	Dutch fleet	42

		Fulco	11
east cliff	106	Fyling Dale	4, 59
East Indiaman	43, 70, 107	Fylingthorpe	4
East Pier	vi, vii, 29, 33		
Edinburgh University	81	Gaskell, Elizabeth	88, 94
Edward I, King	59	Germany	4
Edward II, King	17	ghauts	24
Edwin, King	4, 6, 58	Gibson, Francis	83
Elmet	4, 58	Glover, John	75
Endeavour Wharf	28	Goldsborough	3
English Heritage	4	goldsmith	19
English, Dr Thomas	86	graffiti	47, 97
Esk Bridge	102	Grape Lane	27, 69
Esk Wharf	28	Gray, Walter de	14
Esk, River	1, 2, 3, 24,	Great Barrier Reef	44
	27	Great Book of Whitby	11, 78
Ethelburga, Princess	4	Greengates	27, 69
Etty, Thomas	63, 81	Greenland	28
European Union	40	Greenland whales	27
Evangelical church	93	Greenwich Hospital	43
Everley	14	Grosmont	2, 28
Evesham	7	Guilds	17, 96
		Corpus Christi	17
Fair	16	St Christopher	17
Fairfax, Sir Thomas	61	Guisborough Priory	59
Falklands	106	Gulf of Riga	27
First crusade	11, 58		
fish pier	30	Hackness	11, 12, 14, 58
Fishburn and Brodrick	26	Haggas, Anne	75
Fishburn, Thomas	26	Haggas, Elizabeth	75
fisheries school	106	Haggas, Isabell	75
fishing	73	Haggas, Jane	75
fishing fleet	28, 40, 42, 47	Haggas, John	26, 68, 75
fish-market	ix, 91	Haggas, Jonas	42, 68, 75
Flowergate	64, 93	Haggas, Lawrence	75
Fords	25	Haggas, Mary	75
Forest of Pickering	16	Haggas, Nicholas	75
Fountains Abbey	12	Haggas, Thomas	75
Fox, George	94	Haggersgate House	96
France	59	harbour	viii, ix, 18, 42,
Freeman, Henry	vii, 30, 51		65
French Wars	88	harbour of refuge	29
Friends of Whitby Abbey	11	Harold Godwinson, King	7

Harrison, James	75	Jarrow	4
Harrying of the North	7	John, King	14, 16, 60, 9
Hartlepool	4, 58, 63		
Hastings	7	Kelso	59
Hatfield Chase	6	Kingdom Hall	93
Hemingway, Prof J	86	Knaggs, Francis	42, 70
Henrietta St	vi, 10, 29	Knaggs, Francis	70
Henry I, King	15	Kneller, Sir Godfrey	86
Henry III, King	14, 60		
Henry IV, King	60	Lancaster, Joseph	81
Henry VIII, King	19, 60, 79, 95	Lancasterian Schools	94
herring fleet	54	Langbaurgh wapentake	6, 12
Herrings	17, 25, 27, 46,	Langborne, George	ix
	96	Langborne, Nathaniel	ix
Hexham, abbot John	60	Larpool	vii, 6, 34
high level bridge	25	Lascelles, General Peregrine	62, 86
highway surveyor	95	Lastingham	12
Hilda	4, 5	Laund, Ralph	75
Hilda's abbey	5, 7	Laws of Oléron	41
Hildathorpe College	82	Lay Subsidy	17
Holloway, Rev J	82, 98	Leland, John	18, 42
Holt, John	73	leper hospital	18, 79
Holy Cross guild	17	Letters of Marque	45
Holy Trinity guild	17	liberty	16
Horngarth	30	Life of St Gregory	78
House of Correction	27	lifeboat museum	101
Hudson, George	73	lifeboat station	30, 101
Hugh, Earl of Chester	7, 11	lighthouses	29
Hull	13, 46, 98	Lilla	58
Hull Advertiser	62	Lilla Cross	58
Hull Packet	62	Lincoln, Peter de	17, 41, 4
Humber, River	3, 24, 25		70
Huntrodes, John	26	Lindisfarne	6
Hviti	6	Lindisfarne Gospel	78
		Linskill, Mary	87, 88
Infirmary	79	Literary & Philosophical Society	85
inns and alehouses	48	Littlebeck	93
Insurance	42	*Lives of the Saints*	78
Ipswich	29	Lombardy	17
Iron	72	London	45
		London urine	42
James I, King	61		
Jameson, Storm	88	Malton	3

Manor	15	Odo, Bishop	12
manor courts	30	Ogilby, John	24
Marina	105	Ontario	106
Marine Insurance Society	45	Orkney	69
Marine Society	45	Orm	18
Market	15, 22	Ostend	47
Meaux	13	Oswy, King	4, 5, 58, 107
Mechanics' Institute	85		
Merchant Adventurers	17	Paddock	83
Merchant Shipping Act, 1854	41	Pannett Art Gallery	86
Merchants	16	Pannett, Robert	86
Methodist Church	93	Paul I, Tsar	45, 63, 68
Methodists	94, 97	Pearson, Christopher	70
Middle Earth Tavern	48	Penda, King	4, 58
Middlesbrough	13, 59	Penny Hedge	30
Midwives	80	Pepys, Samuel	107
Mines	74	Percy, William de	7, 11, 12, 58
Missell, Robert	75	personal cargo	44
Mulgrave Castle	16, 60	Peter, Abbot	16
Mussleburgh	17, 59	Pett, Phineas	25
		Pickering	2, 28
Napoleon	63	Pickering to Whitby Railway	85
Napoleon III, Emperor	87	Pickernell, Francis	25
Napoleonic Wars	46, 62	pier	18
navigation	41	pier extensions	30
Navigation Acts	61	piers	31, 32, 61, 64,
Navigation Ordinances	26		101
Navy Board	46	Pilgirmage of Grace	18, 60
new chapel	24, 29, 40, 73,	pirates	42, 46
	82, 84, 98	Plowright, Valentine	84
New Life church	93	Porritt, Jonathan	71
New Quay	viii, 55	port	15
New Zealand	61, 107	Port Stanley	106
Nidderdale	59	Postgate, Fr Nicholas	93, 95
Noble, Mary	42, 70, 73	Presbyterian Church	73
Norsemen	46	Presbyterians	97
North Sea	16	pressgang	46, 48, 61, 88
North York Moors	1	*Prestibi*	6, 14
North York Moors Railway	2	Prestonpans	62
Northallerton	59	Prince Consort	72, 87
Northumberland, Earl of	41, 60	Prince-Bishop of Durham	58
Northumbria	4, 6, 58	Priory of Rumburgh	12
		probate	70

Prussian blue dye	vii	Scarborough	28, 29, 46, 6
Public Baths	85	Scarborough castle	61
		Scarborough, Abbot Roger de	60
Quakers	viii, 27, 43, 68,	schoolmasters	80
	93, 94, 95, 96,	schools	82
	97	Scoresby, William	66
Quays	17, 18	Scoresby, William jnr	44, 81, 98
		Scoresby, William snr	viii, 44
Railway	40, 72, 73, 92	Scotland	13, 16
Recusants	95	Scots	46, 59, 60, (
Reformation	16, 78	Scots+A496 fleet	42
Regatta	48	Scots Presbyterian church	93
Registration of shipping	70	Scott, Gilbert	43
Reinfrid	7, 11, 13, 58	scriptorium	78
Remington, Robert	75	sea-mark	41
Reynolds, Mrs Alice	69	Seamen's Hospital	43, 45
Richard I, King	41	Seamen's Mission	93, 106
Richard II, King	60	Seamen's Sixpence	43
Richard, Abbot	16	seminary priests	61
Richardson & Holt's Bank	74	Serlo	11
Richardson, Mary	69	Seven Years' War	61
Rievaulx	14	Shambles	18
Riga	45	ship yard	105
Robert I, King	13	ship-builders	25, 27
Robin Hood's Bay	30	shipping	69, 74
Roger de Scarborough	13	ships	
Roman Catholics	61	Beagle HMS	86
rope-making	viii, 26	Blith	46
Royal Navy	43	Earl of Pembroke	26
Royal Society	44	Endeavour	26, 44, 10
Rumburgh Priory	20		107
Russia	45, 70	Fishburn	26, 62, 63
Russia Company	63, 69, 71	George	45, 46, 81
Ruswarp	24, 28, 29	Golden Grove	26, 62
Ruswarp bridge	25	Great Neptune	25
Ruswarp Fields	28	John	48
		Opal	viii, 55
sail-cloth	47	Phoenix	44
sail-making	26	A189Rohilla HMHS	64
Saltwick Bay	viii, 52	St Mary Bote	47
Saltwick Nab	18, 64	Superb HMS	62
Sandsend	vii, 59	Thaïs	70
Saunders' Bank	69	Welcome	26
		ship-repair	27, 47

ships' carpenters	viii		99, 101, 106
ship's husband	41	St Michael's church	93, 98
Shipton, Thomas	46	St Ninian's+A494 chapel	93
Shipyards	26	St Ninian's Church	47, 93
Simpson & Chapman bank	69	St Paulinus	4
Simpson, Henry	81	St Peter	5
Simpson, Martin	85, 86	St Peter and St Hilda	7
Siward, Earl of Northumbria	6, 7	St Robert of Newminster	12
Skelton	59	Staithside	62
Skinner St	93, 96	Stakesby	6
Sleights	25, 28	Stamford Bridge	7
Smuggling	45, 48	Stephen, monk	12
Sneaton	45	Stephenson, George	2, 72, 85
Sneaton Castle	82	Stoker, Bram	88
song school	79	Streoneshalh	1, 3, 4, 5,
South African wars	64		6, 58
spa ladder	9	Subscription Library	85
Spanish Armada	60	Suffield	14
Spital Beck	29, 37	surgeons	80
Spital Bridge	viii, 24	Sutcliffe, Frank Meadow	87
Spital Bridge ropewalk	56	Sylvia's Lovers	88
Spring Hill	29	Synod of Whitby	5, 95
Spring Vale	29		
St Aidan	78, 95	Tangier	107
St Andrews, Prior of	60	Tate Hill Pier	29
St Cedd, Priory	12	Tees, River	3, 25
St Gall Monastery	78	Tennyson	40
St Gregory	5	Test Act	80, 95
St Hilda	58, 78, 94, 106	Thames, River	24, 26, 71
St Hilda's Abbey	13, 14, 96	theatres	83
St Hilda's Church	ix, 93, 96, 98,	timber ponds	27
	100	tithe	40
St Hilda's Priory	93	tollbooth	18
St Hilda's Terrace	74	town hall	vi
St John	5	Transit of Venus	107
St John the Baptist	18	tugs	39
St John's Church	93, 96	Turnbull and Scott	27, 38
St Katherine	14	Turnbull's Yard	73
St Mary's Abbey, York	12, 17	Tyne, River	24, 26
St Mary's Church	vi, vii, viii, ix,		
	2, 8, 15, 47,	Unitarian chapel	93
	62, 64, 67, 88	United Reformed Church	93
	93, 96, 97, 98		

Valor Ecclesiasticus	79	Whitby Community College	82
Vaughan, Deborah	68	Whitby County School	82
venture capital	68, 70	Whitby Grammar School	82
Vespasian Psalter	78	Whitby harbour	30
Viaduct	28	Whitby Museum	3, 71, 82, 8!
Victoria Spa	29	Whitby Rock	viii, 40, 101
		Whitby Union Mill Society	73
Walker, John	27, 43, 61, 68	Whitby Whale Oil & Gas Co	28
	94	White Horse and Griffin	48
Walter the Goldsmith	14	Whitehall	vii
war memorials	64	Whitehall shipyard	27, 38
War of American Independence	40, 62	Wilfrid, Bishop of York	5
War of Spanish Succession	61	William I, King	6, 7, 11
Watt, James	69	William II, King	12
Weatherills	86	Winwæd River, battle of	64
Weir	28	Wolfe, General	61
Wesley, John	94	Wolsey, Cardinal	18
West Cliff	2, 73, 90	wool	25, 27
West Cliff Congregational Church	96		
West Pier	vi, 26, 29	Yeoman, Daniel	68
Westerdale	1, 24	Yeoman, Miss Esther	48
Whalers	47	York	6, 12, 14,
Whaling	28, 69, 72, 73,		46, 94
	101	Young, Revd George	73, 82, 85
Wheeldale Moor	3		94, 101
Whitby abbey	21		